Extracts from a Diary
Candika's Journal

Wendy McPherson

DISCLAIMER

Any resemblance to persons living or dead is STRICTLY coincidental. The opinions expressed are those of the characters and should not be confused with the author's. None of the opinions can be considered expert advice. If you have been affected by any of the issues raised in this book, seek advice from an expert.

First published in 2018 by Wendy McPherson
Copyright ©Wendy McPherson. All rights reserved.

All rights reserved. Apart from any permitted use under UK copyright law no part of this publication may be reproduced or transmitted in any form or by any means, electronic or mechanical, including photocopying, recording, or any information, storage or retrieval system without permission in writing from the publisher or under license from the Copyright Licensing Agency Limited. Further details of such licenses (for reprographic reproduction) may be obtained from the Copyright Licensing Agency Ltd, Saffron House, 6-10 Kirby Street, London EC1N 8TS

All illustrations drawn by Wendy McPherson

ISBN: 978-1-909389-21-2

Wendy McPherson

"Only you can make it happen."

- Grandma

Dedication

This book is dedicated to the many people that will have heard about or personally experienced some, many or all of the issues raised within these pages.

My hope is that you will be inspired through this work of fiction, to find some level of shared empathy with the characters and to begin the process of healing.

Also, to the practitioners whose life purpose has been to work empathically and compassionately with young people and the many adults who still carry the unresolved wounds acquired during childhood.

This book is intended to bring about an increase on the value and greater awareness about the range of talk-therapies and other non-chemical healing modalities that aid in individual and collective wellbeing, self-awareness and empowerment.

Wendy McPherson

Extracts from a Diary
Candika's Journal

Contents

Acknowledgements	7
Foreword	8
Introduction	10
SUMMER	11
AUTUMN	48
WINTER	101
SPRING	145
My Self Portrait	148
Personal Affirmation Page	149

Acknowledgements

I would like to thank those who have assisted in the final production of this book. It has been many years since this book was first conceived and a further several years in completing this final draft. This has primarily been because other matters have contrived to suck up my time and also because the time to publish it didn't feel right until now. Well finally it is here and so much thanks goes to Jordan because he continues to be my No1 fan and that's what sons do! To my lifelong friends Sarah and Annie-Mae whose friendship over the years continue to bring laughter and a healthy mix of seriously deep discussion as well as socialization, just enough to help me to not take everything in life so seriously. Whitney who painstakingly combed through the last drafts to bring challenge and endorsement of the issues raised. To Kwame for motivating me to get this project completed. To all the young people who are gifted sparks of light in a world that often tries to dim down your intelligence and creativity while you continue to break free of societal norms. And finally, to the many people who over the years have given me the opportunity to personally experience enough of what this book is about, to be able to write from the heart and not just my head!

Foreword

It has been a great honour and privilege to be part of the *Extracts from a Diary Book One – Candika's Journal*, process with the author, Wendy McPherson.

For those of us who have been blessed enough to share our journeys' with her, know her for her passion, authenticity and her ability to channel her Pharaoh Queen energy and command the attention of a space; Wendy's writing has tapped into that part of us, so many of us hide and exactly what she has brought to the pages of this book, *Extracts from a Diary Book One – Candika's Journal*.

By using her own life experiences and work as a young women's practitioner, Wendy has developed a thought provoking piece to help fill the gap in the self-development market, especially for young women. The journey in *Extracts from a Diary Book One – Candika's Journal* mirrors the gap many of us have when experiencing some of the same pain and trauma Wendy writes about. Candika's Journal encapsulates part of my own story as well as many of my peers and the young women we have worked with. Every woman, from those beginning to learn and understand their womanhood, to those who are in their mastery years, will take something from this gift of love and life.

In our conversations together, Wendy once declared that this story is for those of us who defied the odds and never become who they thought we would be. This is a narrative of rebellion for the women who survive, thrive and go against the theoretical framework.

This is for those of us who turn our pain into passion, taken the hard road through self-discovery in order to put healing first and declaring ourselves free from the cycles of self-hatred, transgenerational trauma and frankly, all the other bull shit we have experience.

Extracts from a Diary Book One – Candika's Journal will help to heal all those who wish to be so.

- Whitney Iles

Introduction

Extracts from a Diary Book One – Candika's Journal is about the many tales and experiences of a sixteen-year-old young woman called Candika. The diary extracts cover a fairly intense period in her life, journaling not only her personal story but also that of her friends and the stories those friends have shared with her. Although this book is a work of fiction, it covers a multitude of issues that many women either personally experience, or know somebody who has.

Extracts from a Diary Book One – Candika's Journal aims to enable discussion about sensitive subject matters including betrayal, child abuse, mother/daughter relationships, aspects of race and identity and many other subject matters while also raising the profile and value of journaling and talk therapy.

Although a work of fiction, it is the author's intention in writing this book, that both readers and talk therapy practitioners may choose to utilize the issues raised within the book to enable: discussion without the need for disclosure especially in group work; exploration of sensitive issues through the lives of the various characters; to provide opportunity to raise awareness about the topics covered through self-awareness, building a personal concept of self-healing and wellbeing; and for developing the quality and skills of empathy.

SUMMER

I swear like a trooper and English Language is my favourite subject. I make words up and love using slang; language is evolutionary and revolutionary.

My name is Candika and these are extracts from my Diary.

July

July 7   I thought he was my soulmate for life, my twin flame, the yang to my ying and the sun to my moon. People will leave you, not because you are too wrong for them, but because you are too right.
Oh for fuck sakes girl, get a grip, I can't even!
I don't want to get poetical right now (Argh! Stop my creative brain right now, this is deeply serious, save the poems for the performances),

Fuck Origin: Early 16th Century: of Germanic origin (compare Swedish dialect focka and Dutch dialect fokkelen); possibly from an Indo-European root meaning 'strike', shared by Latin pugnus 'fist'.

Also commonly used as an intensifier or to denote disdain. Source: Internet search! Other commonly used text and social media versions include FFS, GTFOOH, LMFAO, FY, etc. etc. etc.

I need to be here right now in my secret place, my safe and healing space. This park, these trees, this nature, provides me with the nurturing, privacy and the solitude that I just can't get at home. Here with my diary and my today sorrows. Here in the green and colours of the warmest of summer days and I'm so devastated - Yes DEVASTATED!

Broken up with Luke and I'm besides myself with boundless grief. I feel so rejected. I feel so utterly abandoned. Most of all I feel betrayed. I can't stop thinking about him, wanting, needing to talk to him. I've deleted his number from my phone and blocked his rass from my Snap, Insta... EVERYTHING!

DeleteAbility: v. the ability to let go of what no longer serves your highest good; creating a void that is not for replacing; making space for personal acceptance (see acceptability).

July 9   My thoughts today went something like this:
Sometimes Candika you just need to appreciate that it's

not that you are over enthusiastically expressing yourself and therefore causing people discomfort, and by that I mean in expressing your truth, your feelings, your hurts, baring your very soul. It's just that, well quite frankly, to put it mildly, some people are just simply CONSTIPATED, probably literally, but most definitely metaphorically. Not everybody is an empath, not everyone has the ability to feel or even listen to your pain. So don't worry about displaying moments of vulnerability. Getting it out is more important right about now than holding it all in, even if it means some verbal debris has to come tumbling out with it.

They'll figure it out sooner or later in life how to listen, how to be empathic. In the meantime, the me in you will enjoy watching the Light shine from those beautiful twinkling eyes of yours. It's a tall order trying to Sparkle all the time, sometimes a dimmer switch is the right light for now.

July 12   Saw Luke with his so called 'new girl' today, Janine! Erm....unfuckinbelievable!??
Couldn't he have made a better choice after me than

that? Really? He must prefer 'easy' is all I can say and I feel GUTTED. Totally emotionally cleared out. I thought I knew him better than that but clearly he has gone and lost his damn mind or his mind is being driven by his lower eye! Sense is not so common right? Well that ship must've sailed a while ago for him to make a choice like that. I ain't trying to be petty but errr! Let me go in on that one a bit more with you later, because vex has right got a hold of my pen and I know I can do better than give time and more of my energy over to this. But still...JANINE?

July 14   Louis asked me out today. He's so F.I.N.E. He got accepted into the Uni that he wants to go to, but I'm not sure about him. The boy is gorgeous and he's a genius. They've had to take him on at the age of 16 because there isn't a single school or college that can hold the attention of that human specimen full of intelligence and outright giftedness. Still, I don't want to do a knee-jerk thing, so I told him I would think about it.

Meanwhile back in the seclusion of my sacred space, I am wondering what on earth he sees in me! I feel suspicious, why would he want to get involved with someone like me? Hahaha, 'like me' sounds like I've got low self-esteem and sheeeeet! But I know what I mean, I mean, someone who's got a bag of issues that needs sorting out. And I don't want to come off as para', but do I want to be in a relationship with another 'L'? Can I really be asked to be with another when I feel so down right now over Luke? Hmm, maybe a rebound might do me some good. What do you think? Is what I'm feeling just me being hormonal? I know I'm feeling the need for some one-on-one flesh, but then that feels like I'm just using Louis for sex. Do girls use boys for sex? Is that not okay? The norms of sexual activity these days are not what they used to be, but I don't get any guidance from Mum so I just go by how I feel pretty much these days. It's all guess work at the moment!

I really don't want to bring him into a situation that I haven't yet gotten over, but I just want some male companionship, something healthy whatever that is, and someone fun with a headful of intelligence to top it off. Someone kind of Sapiosexual! I'm gonna sleep on this one (scuse the pun) and put it on the back burner for a while. I'll make my decision when I'm not so vexed. Decisions made in anger are about as fucked up as make up sex!

July 16   Aunt Flo……need to meditate to deal with the tummy cramps, this one is full on this month.

July 17   I can't believe it's over between me and Luke. Not a call, not a face to face meet up, nothing but a note pushed under my bedroom door via my brother.
Faceless bastard…you'll never guess what he has written.
He didn't even have the fuckin guts to tell me to my face. He has actually succeeded in breeding Janine. JA-FUCKING-NINE!?!?!? And she's older than him by three years, with two kids already… It's one thing being prosexual, but she's no-one's Innamorato, she's a sleazy slut!
HOW DO YOU GET TO HAVE 3 KIDS BY AGE 20?
We were always careful, always using a condom and so really, he was only dealing with her so that he could ride that bareback and feel the flesh because I refused

to put myself at risk and BAM…just like that…he's facing fatherhood at the ripe young age of 17. And didn't even have the guts to tell me to my face.

Snake!

I've figured out that he finished with me and more or less had been sleeping with her before that – or the little shit was two-timing me all along. No wonder she kept grinning and skinning up her teeth to me whenever she saw me. She knew that I didn't know what she was up to and she's so disconnected to her self-esteem that she actually doesn't care that she's sleeping with a next woman's man! Has she ever heard about the phrase 'self-esteem'? Does she get off on them kind of 'unavailable men' relationships? Maybe she's too emotionally unavailable and out of touch with herself to even notice how desperate and needy she comes across.

As for him, I can't believe this, what have I done to deserve this? Why must being the good girl always end up in heartache?

Lemmi just give a little pause for thought.

So here's the thing, I'm done! Done with the 'good girl' mentality. Let's see where that takes me, let's see where bringing a bit of risk into this equation called 'life' gets me. It's time for me to start to have some F.U.N.

July 21   I've just ripped up the Luke letter into the tiniest of pieces that my fingertips could rip. I put the pieces into a metal pot and burned them because he doesn't deserve his toxic note to be recycled into someone's paper napkin or paper cup. I want the letter and what we had burnt…ashes to ashes, dust to dust…done with it. Cremated it.

<u>I HATE HIM!</u>

My thoughts while burning the letter made me feel better. Just watching the lit paper shooting tall golden flames and then settling down, its edge curling into burned copper, illuminating the sides of the metal pot. Watching the glow welter down into tiny miniscule flashes of life-like golden nuggets; finally, breathing its last breath to its final cinder.

I want all we had to burn. I want to hate him till I die and I want to die.

I feel so ashamed, so burnt. How can he pick her? Everyone knows she is slack. What is wrong with him? All our dreams dashed in a foolish moment of complete and utter madness. I swear boys are just one big mystery to me.

They just seem to represent abuse – I need to go out and meet some 'good boys', guys that have been raised to have some level of self-respect, compassion for others and some level of understanding about what manhood is. Where are they?

And where are the good men who can teach me how to identify and interact with a good guy. To advise me about what good guys are attracted to and what they are not? Where are the good men who don't hold the 'man-code' above mutual respect and love for healthy human relationships? Where are the good and wise men who can provide guidance and give me the heads up about the mystery surrounding male behaviour. If women are just meant to be loved and understood and men are meant to be respected and understood, then how do we women know when a man has proved worthy of that respect. I've more questions than a Master's degree exam paper. I need an ology's worth of understanding around guy behaviour, because I can honestly say that I just don't understand it!

Luke makes me sick. Hypocrite. All the dreams, all the talking, all the fantasizing together and planning for life after Uni' and now it's totally smashed. He set a car crash in motion that neither of us can walk away from hand-in-hand. In fact, the boy clearly cut off his right arm, hand with it. There can be no reaching out to me even if he had a hand. He took cutting off his nose to spite his face to a whole other level and then there's that mask. That mask dropped quicker than a hooker's knickers when he left me for Janine...Skanky c**t!...Let me search on that one too.

Cunt: Middle English: of Germanic origin; related to Norwegian and Swedish dialect kunta, and Middle Low German, Middle Dutch, and Danish dialect kunte. Looks like the meaning of that one is still up for debate but I'm a go with the Fuck word and state for this entry: commonly used as an intensifier or to denote dis(fuckin)dain.

And Janine...I can't get my head around it. She's a nightmare of a person who calls herself "All Woman". Per-lease, she has abortions like cloudy days in London, so why keep this one? Because she knows deep down that Luke really is a good person. She roped him in just like she did with the rest of them and the fool fell for flesh over and above good common sense and decency…friggin idiot! People like Luke need to understand the difference between a siren and a mermaid!

July 22   MY ENEMY 'N' ME

I had to Befriend my enemy
Her coldness causing pain to me
She suspected I was slowly
Awakening from my apathy
Alive with bursting energy
Eager to prove my ability
Brushed off by her cruel wizardry.
I did not lay down next to him
I only dealt head to head and then
He stripped me of my dignity
And shattered my self-imagery
And then I knelt and let him touch
The crown that I so proudly couched
And then my jewels came tumbling down
And all my confidence crumbled around

The feet of me that bent so low
Could only see that what you sow
Will one day be a signature of
The health of that which is my life
And so my enemy you see
Is very much a part of me
Until the day that I awoke
The chains of bondage I finally broke
To set me on my journey free
I had to befriend my Enemy.

July 23   Clarissa's Mum shared with Clarissa and I last night that she had a light hearted but blatantly candid chat with C's brother about the value of his sperm. This was prompted by the fact that I shared with her the breakup and the situation with Luke expecting a baby. This is what C's Mum said to her brother Jaxon and his spar, Hunter…it went something like this:

> *"Jaxon, and Hunter you may as well listen in on this because I know your Mum will agree. Jaxon, do you know that the most precious thing that you own that is more valuable than all the diamonds, gold and platinum in the*

whole world is your sperm? And I'm going to tell you why. It's because I make up 50% of those genes, and I'm one of the most precious people in your life. And let me tell you this, you may not be fussy about where and in and with whom you procreate, but trust me, I'm particular about who I procreate with. Now we've had the chat about AIDS, sexually transmitted diseases and hygiene, so I'm not going to raise that with you on this occasion, but, here's another reason for wrapping your whacker. If you lack the self-discipline to be selective about who you lay with, just bear in mind that I'm picky and I don't want our DNA to be recreated into some other woman as a result of some fleeting moment, one-night stand or other alternative excuse for not using protection. That's me and your Dad and all your ancestors going in there so please, just think about it."

So here's the thing. I know C's Mum was being playful and I know that she and C's Dad are separated, but she doesn't dis Jaxson's Dad. And C's Dad, who's different from J's, is a great Dad who, from what I see and hear, thinks the world of her.

To be fair, he takes care of J as if he were his own biological son. He proudly introduces J as his son and he doesn't allow anyone to question him on the fact that J is mixed race and he is white as is J's Mum. Makes no difference to him and he goes the extra mile to ensure that J researches and stays connected with the Black side of his family especially as J's own father recently died.

So anyhoo…where the seed goes and where it lays determines the future ancestry of any lineage. I don't know if C's Mum is right in what she's saying to her son but she's got a point, and I've learnt that it's well worth me examining whether I'm ready to face the responsibility that comes with procreation or whether I'm just laying with someone for recreation. We humans have that choice. I guess I for one want to view that choice as a matter for serious consideration.

And WHO would want to put their Mum's, NO….try ancestor's genetics into that old stretched out bag? Luke's Mum and fore-grandmas deserve better than that. She's worked so hard to bring Luke to manhood and has been a Mum to me too when mine wasn't emotionally or physically available to do so. It must be breaking her heart to know that her son places no value on his seed or his legacy.

BUT WAIT! DOES SHE EVEN KNOW? If she does, she must be LIVID. Right now, I'm venomous with hate, but Janine is the snake here. Don't get it twisted!!

July 26   Luke is a lost cause. He has made his bed, literally, and now he will have to lie in it. You lay down with dogs, you get up with fleas!

Janine, is a dam lunatic and she will give him more than a flea's bite and distressing itch. That is a bitch with a bite. He's getting grief for life and you know that that chicken is most definitely gonna come home to roost and I don't want a man who has a lunatic for a baby mother. Pure mama-drama.

And she's such a showboater, I mean her ego roams FREE! It's gonna be a while, if not a lifetime, for her to free up whatever inner pain is locked up behind all of her behaviour. That's a walking time bomb right there!

And you know the type. Her babies aren't evengoing to be out of nappy's and she'll have them wearing the latest designer clothes and trainers, dam, I bet they'll barely be walking properly before those things are put onto their tiny and still forming feet. She's collecting mixed race children like they are a fashion statement and child support like it's a legitimate cash-flow. In fact, that's probably what men are to her, pure cashflow, income and expenses account. That's why she only keeps the babies for the guys who she knows can and most likely will pay up. You know I don't want that kind of life for myself. Ambition won't permit it! But I still can't help feeling that being 'good' is getting me nowhere.

July 27   I feel so mad and sad, so enraged, so cheated on and so used. Did I pick the wrong guy or did the guy make a bad mistake? But why should I have to take the brunt of his mistakes? Well I don't want to and I'm not going to because I'm not going to be punished for someone else's 'mistakes' or irresponsible actions and poor decision making. I had rather be alone than be about that life and so desperate for him and what we'd planned, but allow that, with it comes to that drama, the child is the innocent one, but even still, I think not! I picked up a book off the library shelf today titled The Maxims of Good Discourse by vizier Ptahhotep, 2200 BCE and this is what it said:

> *"If you are a man who leads, calmly hear the speech of one who pleads, and do not stop him from purging his body of that which he planned to tell. A man in distress wants to wash his heart more than that his case be won."*

This is how I feel. I feel like I need to purge my heart out to Luke but I doubt he will even understand, hear or feel me. This girl in distress wants to wash her heart more than anything else, I just want to purge the hurt away. Will it ever happen? Will I ever be free of this monumental disappointment?

July 29 Today I think I'm going to take some time out and have fun. I think I deserve it and Louis seems like a good laugh. It's said that the body heals with play, the mind heals with laughter and the spirit heals with

joy, so why not treat myself to some good healthy laughter? We heal together, right? Last night he said he's made plans but it's a surprise so I'll have to wait and see.
#soexcited-tomorrowtheuniverse!

July 30   Slept with Louis.

August

Aug 1   All I can say is that I'm not too proud of myself right now. We got caught up in the moment. His gorgeousness got the better of me and the fuckability was on point but ugh... I feel so vulnerable now and I just wanted to feel special.

He took us to the Shard for lunch and then a ride on the London Eye. Such a beautiful clear day and school is done for the summer till I start next September and so what else to do but enjoy a beautiful sunny day out with the new man in my life. We went back to his house, parents were both out and so we had the place to ourselves. Still, not a very noble act for someone who knows better and should do better. I made a promise to myself to hold it together, but I broke my own promise. Why does my mind and body seem to do opposing things? I need to understand this. I need to understand the contradictions I experience between my thoughts and my actions. No smiley face for what really should have been a beautiful experience. Not that it wasn't but it wasn't the beautiful experience that I had wanted, and this has happened for me way too soon. Body ready, mind wasn't!

Aug 3   I've to write the truth here. We didn't use a condom.
Why? What was I thinking?
Shit!
The moment just took us and we just did it.
I feel so ashamed. I've put myself at risk of contracting sexually transmitted diseases, infertility or pregnancy. My head is busting, because I'm worried sick. What's going on in that head of mine? I've become as reckless as Luke – how can I allow his pathetic actions to lower my standards? Fuck, I feel like things are getting out of control. I FEEL OUT OF CONTROL. Booked in for a check-up at the clinic in

the morning. Fingers and everything else crossed.

Aug 4   I'm so done with public transport.... don't people know about deodorant? #humming #putrid #unhygienic #odoriferous or stinking to high heaven! Anyways, I've just returned home from my check-up appointment. They issued me with antibiotics as I tested positive for Chlamydia. I don't even know if that's from Luke or newly from Louis, but I'm going to have to tell Louis, it's only fair. Damnnn! I've put my fertility at risk and now I've got to wait a further week to get my HIV/Aids results. I'm frightened. What if I've got AIDs? I may not like my life right now, I may not be proud of myself right now, but I DON'T WANT TO DIE. I feel so much regret and I feel so disappointed in myself. It's like every hurtful thing that I'm feeling about Luke I'm duplicating myself like I believe I deserve to feel it again twice over. It's almost like I am punishing myself for my poor choices. In life, we can prepare to fail or prepare to succeed. I must do better for myself. This is not good enough. This is not how I want to manage my life now or in the future.

Aug 7   I can't sleep, can't eat, can't talk. I should be out having fun and enjoying this good weather but I'm having a mindfuck over this waiting and it's leaving me feeling nothing less than completely drained of all motivation to do anything. I've been using the time to busy myself by tidying my room and getting rid of school books I no longer need. A major declutter in my estimation. I've watched them programmes about hoarders. I mean it's one thing to be a collector of things, but the ones I've seen on those tv programmes aren't collectors of things of evidential value. I mean the items are obviously of value to them, but whenever it comes to letting go of what appears to be crap, they get all hyper-anxious and then you see their trauma playing out and they're all in a turmoil. I've seen the clutter up to the height of the ceiling and it's like every nook and cranny of their home is crammed with stuff. I don't understand it personally but it does seem to me like some kind of mental health situation. So I'm not judging the hoarder or their hoarding habit, but it must be something to do with fears about letting go and needing to feel in control.

So while decluttering I also got caught up reminiscing over my years in senior school and the situation I now find myself in has just created such a mental block that I can't even think about the future, what it looks like or where I'll even be in a year's time. I don't want to hear anything about crying over spilt milk but that's how I'm feeling right now, and I know I beat myself up more than anyone else. I feel in Pain.

P A I N

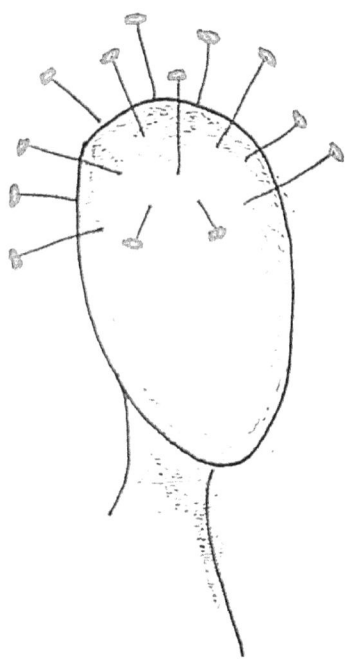

Aug 10   PAIN

It's like when every single shaft of hair

on the top of my head

nearest to my forehead

stands erect.

It's like when my skin contracts

Tightly embracing my bones within

And

Those bones remain on Ice

on a hot summer's day.

It's spiky all over and

it makes me feel unable to touch it

because it's knife edge sharp

and so I know if I do,

I'll feel it's cruel slice

And

It feels like my skull has been turned

inside out so that

that which is within is totally exposed.

It feels like I can feel

every electromagnetic charge

exploding inside my head and in so doing

>it paralyses my thoughts.
>It's like when I know I'm going to cry,
>but I can't make a sound,
>so the tears trip over my cheeks
>In Silence.

Aug 12 I think I'm pregnant.
I can't remember ever being late and it is almost midnight.
'Aunt Flo' hasn't arrived and I'm freaking the fuck out.
Fuck Fuck Fuck and Fuckin Fuck.

Aug 13 I attended an appointment back at the clinic to get a pregnancy test and to pick up my other results.
I've tested positive.
I'm pregnant.
I'm fucked and my life's officially over and a mess.
I was coming back from the clinic, standing at the bus stop and this woman was standing there. An angel must've sent her.
I was crying and unsuccessfully trying to hide the

fact, so she handed me a tissue and looked at me as if to say she understood. She's the first person in my life I've connected with like that. No words, just a look that told me she knew. An understanding exchanged with a tissue. There was a calmness about her. She was not afraid of me or my tears. She didn't break eye contact with me as I gave her my best threatening "back-off-n-keep-out-of-my-business" look. I found myself beginning to tell her my story. I don't know why, there was just this instant connection and it drew me to her. Even though I cursed and screwed up my face, she showed no offence. She came with no judgement. She just stuck in there with me to hear my story. I feel absolutely exhausted, drained, depleted, devoid, EMPTIED.

Will share more tomorrow.

TEARS.

Aug 14   Eva is a shapely woman, toned and lean, athletic but not muscular. She has the darkest of brown eyes, almost black. Her pupils and iris are one tone of black and brown. Deep pools of midnight hiding wise words and thoughts. Aunt Eva and those eyes.

I couldn't look at those eyes while I talked my story. As soft and as sympathetic as they were, I felt ashamed. I knew I was in the presence of someone special and I think I felt unworthy of her. I told her I didn't want to die. That I was afraid to tell my parents what I was going through. I wanted her to be the mother that I don't have, the mother that listened and be the confidant of my experience and to feel safe speaking my truth. I told her I was too afraid to go through with an abortion. That I didn't have anyone I could trust and help me through such an ordeal.

That's why I refer to her as Aunt, she felt like family - not a stranger, it was that instant connection and that older woman vibe.

She felt like someone who knew my soul, someone to abandon my inhibitions with, someone who was not easily offended by the mistakes I made as immature as they may've seemed.

I'm so easily judged in my household but in that moment with her, I felt able to be released from the bondage of guilt and personal betrayal that have experienced in life.

It was the feeling of being at ease, like when I sink into my bath and submerge under the water level hearing only the sounds of my own breathing.

You know what, I know what it was, it was just simply fucking EASY!

Absent of all of the complications that other adults in my life always brought to the discussion table. She made it easy for me to bring to the surface stuff I haven't yet even allowed myself to hear let alone anyone else.

Yes, it was easy, I just flowed and my thoughts began to rush through me as if for the first time some real reason to talk had just presented itself to me.

She made it easy for me to articulate in my way, in my language, in my tone and in my current state of distress.

She made it easy for me to try to address my situation like making a plea to a judge to be heard, to achieve a kind of justice where an injustice had been silenced.

She made it easy for me to mourn what I knew was a dream and a life I had been planning for. And she made it easy for me to arrive at a temporary decision that what happens next is my choice based on what I believe is right for me at this current moment in time. I've made no decisions.

Aug 15 The Sun is Always Shining, but sometimes there are just more clouds in its way.

Aug 16 Went back to the Advisory clinic for advice. I don't know if I want to keep it.
How can I?
What are my options?
What the fuck should I do?

Aug 17 Before I got onto the bus that day I met Eva, she asked me if I wanted to talk some more and at the same time help other young women, that I could come to a girl's group she ran near her home. She gave me her business card. I've never been given anyone's business card before, I thought that was just for business people!! But I mean business and that business right now is my life and that of my baby's.
Eva has been adopted by me as an 'Aunt', so she's fam' now. When I got onto the bus I looked down at

her through the upper deck window and I knew I was going to see her again. While looking up at me she gave me the 'call me' signal and as sad as I was I nodded a 'yes'. Eva had something written on the card, it read:

"You know what, the sun is always shining, it's just that on some days there are more clouds in its way."

Aug 18   My head is busting.
I feel so alone.
No-one to talk to.
So much for summer
So much for term break.
Sad face. More tears.
☹

Aug 19   #video call with Eva.

Aug 20   From that first experience at the bus stop, Eva taught me what listening is truly about. Hers is solid listening. She listened with her body, her mind and spirit. No interruptions. Even though I felt ashamed, it wasn't because of her. I felt no judgement from her and I began to ease up and free myself from the chains of secrecy to a level of freedom that allowed me to share my burdens, thoughts and feelings.

I feel so much lighter, less alone, less frightened. I feel like I'm gaining some sense of normality. At least my head doesn't feel so prickly. I feel less desperate and less despair. I feel like there's some hope. I can feel again. I've found someone I can TRUST.

SHAME (n.)

Old English *scamu, sceomu* "feeling of guilt or disgrace; confusion caused by shame; disgrace, dishonour, insult, loss of esteem or reputation; shameful circumstance, what brings disgrace; modesty; private parts," from Proto-Germanic **skamo* (source also of Old Saxon *skama*, Old Norse *skömm*, Swedish *skam*, Old Frisian *scome*, Dutch *schaamte*, Old High German *scama*, German *Scham*). The best guess is that this is from PIE **skem-*, from **kem-* "to cover" (covering oneself being a common expression of shame).

Aug 23 The wind whispers and waves of the summer flowers sweet fragrance blends within the gentle breeze that seeks to caress the skin of a young woman whose heart heaves a heavy sigh as she reflects over the months gone by. And the heat of the noonday sun envelopes her skin like a blanket that gradually emulates a warmth, which replaces the synthetic cold that had taken a-grip. And should she move, a draught of bitterness comes to torment her and so she remains perfectly still; not moving lest the door from the past should open a wound that has failed to heal. Yet, if she moved in a certain direction, the past would equally serve to remind her of good times as much as the so called bad.

So she creates the antidote, which counteracts the poison of negative thoughts and feelings. She remembers one who loves, cares, forgives, exudes happiness. She remembers the power found in peace, love and hope. She remembers that she has all of these hidden treasures buried deep inside the heart of her. The barriers of fear, rejection and isolation tumble. The dominant forces that teach the lies that this is life's lot disperse when she delves into the treasure chest.

She remembers that love has the ability to annihilate the corrosive energy of anger that only serves to strangle every opportunity to progress from the pain of the past. She understands that to live from day-to-day is to savour each bite of life's succulent meal. And so, she devours every opportunity that enables her to recover from the pain of the past.

Aug 25   Did I mention already? I don't think I did but this is too important not to. My AIDs/HIV results came back negative.

Halla fuckin loolyah! ☺

Aug 27   My boobs are growing and I feel sick and look wrecked for being so tired. I've been laid low because I'm so nauseous. I'm having pregnancy rage, what fool called it morning sickness? I've got this fight for normality all fucking day. I can't stand the sight and smell of raw meat, it makes me heave and the nausea is tiring me out. The baby is literally the size of a lentil and whilst the world around me can't see a thing one bit of activity that's being noticed in the house is my excessive journeys to the loo. This is emotional blackmail and physical torture! How can something so tiny cause so much chaos? I've only told one person and that's him. He's not bothered either way what I do. I don't think he's got a clue about the reality of trying to raise a child. I'm only 16. I feel as if my hopes and dreams are sliding away from me but I am where I am.

I already feel like a Mum. Well kinda. Well, what I mean is that how can I kill the very thing that I want to protect. But how can I let this thing inside of me run the rest of my life? I'm sooo confused. I'm in utter turmoil. This is not what I planned and this is not what I want, but…?

#screwface

Aug 29   Called Eva again today. Felt a bit anxious, it's been 10 days since we last spoke. She remembered me! It feels so easy talking to her. Why is it so easy to talk to her? Thinking about it, I put it down to a number of things, things that I found important and I want to structure this a bit, because this is for my own growth:

- She remembered my name
- She said that she respected me for calling her because it's a big step
- She told me that she has no interest in judging me for what I've done to myself or what I'm currently doing
- She told me that her main concern is for my health and well-being on every level. I asked her what that meant, and she explained it as a physical, mental, emotional and academic one too.
- She wasn't going on like those other people who only work with you so that they can collect their paper at the end of the month, those types don't really care, they're not invested in my personal wellbeing, just their own.
- She asked me what my purpose in life is,

who I thought I was and where I wanted be in life in the next 5 to 10 years' time?

Well after that question I was gobsmacked. For the first time in my life, someone is showing a real interest, with a passion, in me for who I was and for who I could become. I know I keep saying it, but I feel like life is looking up! She's showing me not to be deterred by my circumstances and to remain focused on the vision I had for my future regardless. Good Night!

Aug 30 — Woke up with my own name – Candika – on my lips. It's a Sanskrit name meaning Fierce Goddess. I'm just a young woman wanting to share her thoughts and feelings with young women like her. Someone I met, thank the Universe, told me that talking helps, *but only* if it's honest and focused on change for the better. I've learnt and want others like me to learn, that you're not alone even though you might feel alone in the pit. I dreamt about all of the things I've done to feed the sadness and the anger: shoplifting, violence, sex, alcohol, all kinds of stuff but it never really goes away for long, more like a nightmare really. Since I met Eva my thinking has begun to change. Anyway, time to get up and get out, more about Eva later, I'll leave you dear diary with my pen and pending thoughts.

AUTUMN

September

Sept 6   Left my diary too long, and let the madness build up like puss in my head.

Eva has suggested that I keep a journal to capture the content of my journey. When I told her I already kept one, she smiled that beautiful beaming smile of hers. We went on to discuss how important the journal has become for me to help sort through and unfilter my thoughts.

Anyway, I'm back now and eager to talk about Aunt Eva. She represents for me the kind of tight family that every child should have and too many of us don't; instead we get adults who are more screwed up than us! We've kids trying to raise kids, competing with us like kids and trying to resolve issues in juvenile ways.

Eva's a straight talker and she has the same anger in her that I have. I can feel it. The only difference is that she's at peace with her rage, she says, "Candika, I'm the master of my rage not the other way around, the beast works for me."

Extracts from a Diary: Candika's Journal

I dreamt about her last night. She looked radiant, healthy, glowing with goodness and she was holding this basket full of fruit and there were children running in circles around her, jumping up and tiny hands trying to grasp at the fruit. I shared the dream with her and she laughed and said, "Young lady, the fruit's knowledge, affection, support and love, and you get access to them by striving to be the best that you can be." She's always stating "be the best that you can be." Aunt Eva is helping me to see life differently.

I can't wait for our next session ☺.

The best part of receiving is found first in the giving and being thankful for what I already have. I'm noticing what already is good and wonderful about my life. It's not easy given the current situation, but as Eva quite rightly stated, it can be done.

Sept 9   Went to Aunt Eva's session and did something for the first time tonight. It was amazing. First I wanted to cry, then I was angry with her, then I felt a sense of relief after I went in the TRUTH

CHAIR.

What is the *Truth Chair*? The Truth Chair is placed into the middle of the circle that we sit around. It's intentionally placed there. Everyone can see it and when you sit on it, everyone sees you on all sides. Sitting in a complete circle all energy is held within the circular gathering of us girls, like when we all link hands and sit in silence. You can feel the heat being turned up, this is pure energy coming from within us.

The Truth Chair sits in the centre of the circle, drawing us, calling us to release deeply held beliefs, experiences and feelings. It calls us to release our truth. When I'm in the Truth Chair I am releasing My Truth!

I sat, watched and listened to the other girls, week after week as they talked through their feelings. I watched them and just by listening to them I've become transformed, building up my confidence to the point that I can't wait to gain the courage to sit in the Truth Chair in order to step closer to personal and liberating healing.

The Truth Chair was my number one enemy when we were first introduced and as I began to understand why I hated it, I also understood that the challenge of talking my stuff was to be my biggest challenge and also the pathway to being my greatest liberator. I had never come across such a barrier that, at the very same time, was also my big opportunity. I knew that to get free of past experiences that bound me up in anger, torment, sadness and sorrow, I needed to be fearless and talk them out. But the fear of being judged and criticised by others was holding me back. So that night I took the first step and had my first taste of emotional freedom. Never before have I experienced talking about my feelings or being listened to by people who wanted to hear about how I felt. Wanting to hear about how I felt because they too wanted to enable and assist me in my healing process. I realise now that I've a Truth Chair inside of me and that whenever I want to share how I'm feeling I can ask myself and tell myself anytime I want to. This diary is my listening audience. This is Candika's Journal and

I thank you for L.I.S.T.E.N.I.N.G.

Tired now. Going to get a good sleep tonight! Those who do the work, the deep work, reap rewards and one of those rewards feels like freedom.

Sept 10   Coming from a large family isn't all it's cracked up to be. People who've smaller families must have it all good because mine just create so much madness in my life.

Sept 11   Too many secrets that stay bundled up in the back of a choked throat of those who daren't speak them. I want to burn them all, every single dirty secret that hangs silently in the air, invisible but we all know they're there, we just hope no-one else can see them. The emperor thinks he has new clothes, yet he stands naked in his foolish illusion pretending that no-one can see his nakedness. Denial is a strange thing.

Eva says that those secrets reveal themselves in different ways. She says that our behaviour can betray it. For example, sometimes I can get so angry about the smallest of things. The rage I feel inside is so unbearable that I've to spit it out like it's poison. The only thing is that I end up frightening and pushing away the people around me. They just don't understand that I'm not really raging at them but instead at the mountain of things that I've been through. Even worse, I've not understood this for myself up until now.

Eva says this is sometimes called 'dysfunctional' behaviour. I needed to look up the word dysfunctional and in my dictionary, it means: *unable to deal adequately with normal social relations*. Eva also says that the space in the Truth Chair, hard as it may be, is my very own space to download my thoughts and feelings in a safe and non-judgemental space.

When you're insecure, when you've been abandoned and neglected, been told lies to, threatened and made to feel unsafe AND told to keep someone else's secrets OR ELSE, you don't feel like you've got anywhere to run or anyone to turn to and then you just feel L.O.N.E.L.Y.

Upon the advice of Aunt Eva, I've created my

own game of learning new words or using positive and empowering words by creating acronyms. This helps me to express myself through this wordplay and it's also broadening my vocabulary. I want to find more than one word to express my feelings so where I feel the need to I'll do a bit of wordplay to get my feelings out just like this:

Lost

Outcast

Neglected

Empty

Left

Y?

It's better than cussing all the time, right? The cussing may give me a short term energetic relief, but it doesn't change my internal future response to certain situations that seem to trigger the same cycle of behaviours that I absolutely know are unwanted. I want change and I'm committed to changing. I want to change the way I respond; I want to break cycles of my reactionary behaviour. I want to change my language and be constructive in my choice of words. I want to know that it's ok not to respond straight away with regretful statements and that to give pause for thought isn't a sign of weakness. I want to be articulate and that's because I want to be the expression of all that is good about and within me. I want to be my own good ambassador and represent myself in a way that doesn't undermine and disadvantage me and that gives me the best chance to advance. And I want to learn these skills in the best way I can, without cutting corners and without compromising my goal to grow.

I own and take responsibility for myself. I'm my best ticket out of these circumstances because at the end of the day, only I can make it happen. I've met some great people that are equally committed to joining me on this current journey, primarily because they have been as up front with me about wanting positive change in themselves too.

It's a crime against young people that adults in this world go around pretending all is well and that by not dealing with their own shit they'd rather it spills out like vomit onto their own flesh and blood rather than to take responsibility and be held to account for their actions. At the very least get some fuckin help! Is it so painful for you adults to look at your own face in the mirror? Mirror for me means me becoming:

Mature

Invincible

Responsible

Reasonable

Owning it and so Over it

Wiser

I'm reminded constantly of my own shame, anger, hatred, loneliness and grief at not being able to have the right to have a 'normal' childhood. To just be able to 'be' but the boundaries that define what's a normal childhood have been incrementally shifting over the years and the emotional suffering has moved more and more to a physical and violent one.

To be a young person and not having to worry about sitting on my own uncle's lap for fear of his hands wandering off into places he knows he shouldn't touch, should not be a normal fear for us! Even women aren't off limits when it comes to abuse. I know enough of my male friends who've shared stories of how they lost their virginity before the legal age with women old enough to be their aunt. It's RAPE! These boys have been RAPED!

My rage is a powerful energy, which when unleashed makes me feel that it's the only real lease of life I've left within me, the only honest and pure thing that I can display without being ignored! My rage is the only thing I can honestly feel, because I can't feel happiness, love, an honest caress or hug. I can't laugh, dance, sing or skip for long because when I start to show displays of what I feel to be uplifting moments of happiness, it gets crushed, stamped out, punched out, knocked out, slapped out of me, replaced with an enforced unhappiness. An unhappiness that doesn't come from me nor belongs to me.

Other people's rage is forced down my throat and mixed with toxic words drunk down in gulps to the pit of my stomach because no matter what I do, it just isn't good enough. I speak no, see no, hear no evil, because if I do, I receive nothing but punishment, ignorance and belittling responses from those who call themselves adults.

My rage is my cathartic release. When my rage emerges from the pit, her pit, and his, their rages ascends in unity with mine. A collision of universal rage. I can't see. All goes back to black when my rage unravels itself upon my victims. When I get into fights, I can't feel my sense of touch or sight. It all goes numb, it all fades to black. Blind rage is REAL people.

I'm FEARLESS in my rage and my aim is to squeeze every last drop of toxic anger out from within me, so don't poke me, don't provoke me to anger. I don't like it when I get mad. I'm slow to anger but when I pop I feel that power surge through me; a release of pent up emotion.

I both love and hate it.

Don't trap me, don't back me into a corner because I like options and I'll always find a way out but it's not necessarily my preferred choice. And I'll always find a way out! I'm not an idiot, I'm not indecisive when enraged but I need choices and the adults around me haven't been able to assist me, not until Eva that is.

So when you see me, see ME.

When I talk, hear ME.

Don't walk around me when you see me crying in the street because I've just been made homeless escaping another dirty episode of abuse. I want to know; I need to know why all of this is happening to me?

Hear my cries for help, stop ignoring the signs, don't ignore. I can't hold this back anymore, I can't do it any longer because I no longer feel ashamed, guilty or entirely responsible for all that has happened to me. My responsibility lies with what happens to me now and next.

My years of silence is now over and I most certainly am NOT ALONE.

#feelingempowered.

Sept 14 — Went to Eva's Girls Group (Double G!). Her dress sense is interesting and she has many styles. She's a stylish woman but not a fashion victim. She looks regal, respectful. I know I can't afford those kind of quality clothes, and there's plenty of time for earning that kind of money but I know I can get them cheaper. When I asked Eva where she gets her clothes from, she says she gets some of them made but some are also very affordable, she 'jazzez' them up with accessories and good shoes.

Eva says good quality shoes are far more important than quality clothes because those small digits at the end of her feet need enough comfort and support to carry her on through this life. So, she doesn't mess around when it comes to footwear and she'll pay for comfort and style for her feet from each purchase. She says she only buys the best that she can afford because quality should never come at the price of not being able to pay her bills or put food on her table. That's really given me something to think about.

Eva has raised my self-awareness around what I wear and how that either portrays who I really am or who I'm trying to be. Am I trying to be the name on the label or me? When I look at those low batty trouser wearing boys (maybe - in their Giuseppe trainers, Gucci belts, Armani Jeans and Rolex watches, I'm disgusted...who are they trying to be? I listened to a programme the other night and it was about rap, grime and drill artists and how they've NEVER lived the life that they chat about let alone ever seen or held a gun. Unfortunately, their negative lyrics seem to penetrate deep into the mandem around my endz. They're trying desperately to gain credit by acting out for real what they hear them rappers chat about. I ain't got time for that kinda man but I love my people and I have a deep urge for them to wake up from the illusions of grandeur they've been programmed to aspire to.

Sept 15   This is HUGE facts right here. I need to link up with some of my boys and see what their thoughts and views are about this. Essentially, these so-called artists are creating an illusionary lifestyle. Nobody's talking about how they're heavily subsidised and how their income goes straight back into the system through the cars, the clothes, the bling, the drink and drugs. Who're the real beneficiaries? What is it that they are really after, the celebrity, the notoriety? Is that a beg for attention, a cry for some kind of love and from who? Let me leave this one, this topic for another time.

Sept 16   At Double G, Eva held my hands when I arrived to warm them up, winter has arrived early this autumn and my hands weren't prepared for the sudden drop in temperature! Her hands are so soft. Her nails, all her own, clean and manicured. It tells me that she likes to pay even the smallest of attention to her hygiene (Eva taught us about this) and that she takes time out for herself as a demonstration of love for herself. She was wearing a different hairstyle tonight. She likes to wear it in a variety of ways. She says that to be creative with ourselves at this young age helps us to practice using different aspects of our character or personality. As an older woman, Eva says that changing her hairstyle or dress code all forms part of her creative expression. She says she's past the point of caring what society dictates are the norms for hair, clothes and standards of outward appearances. She always emphasises the 'inner glow' as she calls it, and the importance of paying more attention to our inner self. However, she has taught me to embrace my ALL and to be fearless in being comfortable within my own skin and natural as well as my made-up make-up face! She says that when we define who we are nobody else gets to apply a label, that's my right and mine alone.

Creativity is Fun ☺

> *The name Eva means: Latin form of Eve, comes from Hebrew and means to breathe or to live.*

Eva wears an Ankh ☥ on a chain around her neck. I asked her tonight what the symbol means, she said that it has relevance to the meaning of her name and that Ankh ☥ means 'Life'. She said that the Ankh ☥ was a sacred symbol to the ancient Egyptians (this is actually the land of Ancient Kemet – the land of the Black people, the Africans – which the Greeks later renamed Egypt) and is known as the 'original cross'. This symbol ☥ stands for life or living and forms part of the Egyptian words that mean Health and Happiness. This is why it's often referred to as the 'Key of Life'.

Eva says that she believes her purpose in life is to heal and to cause happiness or joy within others. I think I'd like to believe that I could achieve this sometime soon in my own life. Happy is good for me and I haven't had much of it so my time has to be NOW. Surely 'now' time is the only time reality…yesterday is gone and the next minute is always a minute away. So the only real time is NOW.

N

N ☺ W

W

Sept 17 I met some new girls last night, it was the end of a series of meetings that Eva runs to help young women deconstruct, discuss and rebuild their understanding about who they are. She calls it a 'process'. It's nothing like anything I've ever been to before. Some girl there was talking about suicide. She'd tried to kill herself. I can't get my head around that, listening to her off-load about it, it shook me to my core. Although I feel like my life's in bad shape, I don't want to end it. Not now anyway being so over Luke. I'm not feeling to take me off the planet right now. She described herself as a 'self-harmer' and I had never heard of that before. She really didn't like herself. I've never wanted to harm myself, I can't take physical pain but Eva pointed out to me later that we can self-harm in different ways, ways that cause mental pain or by using drugs or abusing substances that could cause death. I did relate to her loneliness and I remembered at that point wanting to run away from home. I do remember putting scissors to my belly thinking I could end it but it was the pain that stopped me.

I can't do pain!

Sept 18   You see I can't do pain because of the beatings. Mother has in her own distorted and twisted way of punishing me which in my mind is not just physical abuse but also mental. Sometimes I don't think she's in her right mind, I now know why. She was raised in violence and she was abducted and severely abused as a child. Eva explained this to me in my counselling session today. Right now, this night, I'm too drained to go through with writing what I now know. Will write more about it tomorrow.

Sept 19 Remember I talked about Double G being a process? Eva explained that my mother may benefit from going through a process where she can begin to talk about her childhood experiences. She said that this would help her to make sense of how those past experiences currently cause her to behave the way she does at times. She warned that it might be very hard for Mum to change her ways and treat me differently from the way she was treated in her childhood. She said that people only change if they are ready and willing. It's given me something to mull over. I had never considered Mum having her own therapy. I can't see her sitting let alone talking in the Truth Chair. I had like to be a fly on the wall for that!

Sept 20 I don't want to be my mother and treat my children the way she treated me. Old ways have to stop with me and new ways and behaviours have to start with me. Them old ways end with this generation. My new ways will pave the way moving forward and that's not just about me as a parent, but more importantly me as a person. My mother didn't become the way she is because she's a parent, she was that way before I came along. Now when I arrived on the planet, I became the focal point for her to offload and project her inner rage onto!! That's not adult, not mature, not fair and not good parenting. That blue-print pattern of behaviour may be her template for parenting, but most definitely isn't going to be mine. I don't even want to wait to become a parent before I tackle my issues and that's why I, even if nobody else is, am proud I'm taking a step toward my personal change TODAY:

Topical

Overstanding

Developing

Adult

Y? Because I matter ☺

Sept 23   One of the girls expressed that she didn't feel like her mother was her mother. She was sitting in the Truth Chair and Eva was helping her to understand these feelings. She was recalling asking her Mum when she was thirteen whether her Mum was her real Mum. Just listening to her story began to make me feel depressed and sad. I need to unpack those feelings. Eva suggests I don't ignore or suppress what I'm feeling when others share, but that I, at the very least, acknowledge them. Writing this down is my acknowledgment, unpacking it further is my commitment.

Sept 24

Sometimes I don't believe that someone who's supposed to love you is supposed to treat you the way I'm treated. I can never be good enough, always under pressure to be the good child, perfect and always on display at family gatherings. If only they knew what this good girl has now done to herself, it would shatter their illusion.

But to whose cost but my own. ☹ I've to now hold up the mirror to my own face and reflect on what I've done and how and why. As a child, I was well dressed, well fed and bullied.

BULLEEEEEEEEED. I kept that a secret. Bullied by my siblings, bullied at school and most of all bullied by my parents. How confusing can it be to be so nicely provided for yet treated so badly? How confusing! How can someone who claims to love you also be your bully? How can someone who feeds you with one hand, deny you with the other just as fast? How can someone embrace you and hold your hand with the same hands that beat you? What pain has a parent endured to be able to handle their child so cruelly in return? For whom am I really taking punishment for? And when will it all end and how?

So many unanswered questions.

I'm exhausted.

Sept 26   Went to Double G and we talked about Chlamydia. If untreated it can lead to infertility and unlike some other infections, you can get it and not even know it. Chlamydia is a common sexually transmitted infection and is passed on through unprotected sex. Symptoms include pain when peeing, unusual discharge, men can get pain and swelling in their balls and women can get bleeding after sex or between periods. They've even got chlamydia testing kits you can do at home and it's treated with antibiotics. Prevention is using a condom and not sharing sex toys. There's more to it but for the journal this is my recall and there's lots more information at school, the GP and of course the internet.

Thank you to me for getting it checked out asap!

Sept 27   I find myself looking forward to going to Double G now. It's a drop-in style service so you can go when you need to. I'm less shy about talking and sharing my stuff. The more we talk, the more I understand that I'm not alone in my life. We've more in common than we think. We've all agreed to a code of conduct and we're all of the same understanding that what we share might be talked about, we can't gag each other like we're in the secret service! So, I do think about what I'm sharing and that's part of the freedom that comes with sharing. Just talking about it brings a release and actually more time is spent talking about understanding and taking the discussion to a more solution focussed one. Letting go of 'secrets' has become the biggest single liberating act of self-love. I'm caring less about people knowing and caring more about me growing ☺

Sept 28   Some of the girls at Double G have been in trouble with the police and even thrown out of school, all that stuff. I think that they've got it much harder than me and they've really turned their lives around using the knowledge that Eva has given to us. But most of all it's the opportunity to talk to each other about our life issues that we seem to find ourselves doing most of the time. Eva doesn't drive the discussion, it's us girls. Eva only jumps in if we need her input or if it looks like we've ground ourselves into a corner, which usually causes us to feel frustrated or we start acting out our dysfunctional ways. But we've Eva to keep us on track and we remind ourselves at the beginning of each session what our group boundaries are that we agreed to keep. Setting these boundaries have helped us to understand what it is to set expected standards of behaviour for each other. Eva has discussed with us the concepts of standards, values, beliefs and how they inform, whether for the good or otherwise, our thoughts, behaviours and judgements and whether they serve us well or not.

Sept 30   I feel safe at Double G. I got really close to Torrie tonight. She's 18 and is being bashed about by her father and her brothers who're touching her up and have done so since she was 13! What's fuckin wrong with these people?!? It seems like they're everywhere! As she told us her story for the first time, I felt so sad and angry inside and then my own memories came up. I haven't shared that with the group yet, too much other epic shit that I'm trying to deal with.

I had real contact shame hearing Torrie's story, especially when she went into the details. I felt like if I spoke the anger would be the only thing left standing in the room, do you feel me on this? I know you know what I mean, when the head is so tight, the images, the sounds, smells from the past are all in the present moment and all you want to do is leave planet Earth. And then after the rage must come the calm, every week somebody in our group is storming out after losing it, not wanting to break the standards, not wanting to offend. But we begin to have even more understanding about each other's situations. Eva calls this the introductory of the empath. Where before we were desensitised by our traumas, we're now beginning to become sensitive again. The trick is to not to allow the emotions expressed by others to control our own, but that's proving harder in practice right now because I'm still on the edge of revealing my own rage. I know when I take that leap I'll develop wings on the way down and then up and up I'll go.

Olivia spoke tonight about being mixed race. She spoke from the heart. Her Mum is black and her Dad is white. Olivia is fair and you can tell she's got Black in her but she looks more unusual than other mixed race girls. Olivia has green hazel eyes and her hair is light brown curly hair. She has inherited her mother's African hips and thighs and she has a natural inclination toward Black culture because that's what she was raised in. Olivia's father died while she was yet to be born. He died in the Iraq War.

Olivia is actually a friend of mine and I introduced her to Double G after we had one of our heart to heart talks. We became friends at school in Year 10 and have been tight ever since. Up until that point, Olivia had got herself, well actually one of her friends, mixed up in some extremist group and she felt that she had to make a decision to cut her off and make other friend choices. She cut off her friend, Harper, when Harper didn't take kindly to Olivia's ultimatum: choose me or them. Harper did what Harper always liked to do, which was to choose to walk on the wilder side of life. When I approached Olivia at school, she was isolated and without any friends. When I asked her what'd happened she described the situation with Harper and said her friend showed no love toward her and that she felt uncomfortable because she was 'different' from the others and that in addition to their extremist views, she felt outside of the clique because of it. Me being me, I hate to see people alone because I know what it's to feel lonely. So I invited Olivia to hang out with me, Harper became history and we've been tight ever since. Most of what I write in this journal, Olivia knows.

Olivia taught me so much about what it's to be considered 'different'. Being mixed race, she has had to deal with difference all of her life but tonight she poured her heart out about how this has impacted upon her and how she was treated by other people from a very young age. I could relate to her but my difference is to do with me being dyslexic. I thought I was stupid, stupid, stupid and certainly hid my difference by being late for classes that required me to read and write, which was most times. If I couldn't do a lateness, I pulled a sicky and would often have the school office call my Mum to come and get me or I caused myself an injury in order to opt out of certain classes.

In Year 5 this behaviour pattern of mine was monitored by the Special Educational Needs teacher at my school. My SEN teacher, Ariana, and I began having meetings during the school day and eventually we had a meeting with Mum where it was agreed and permission given that I had be assessed. When Mum and I recalled the conversation years later, she did say that she was concerned that I was being labelled with a mental illness. But dyslexia is nothing like a mental illness, it's just seeing the world in many ways differently in terms of letters and numbers.

After the assessment, it was 100% conclusive that I had been diagnosed as Dyslexic. I wasn't stupid, I just experienced words and reading differently. Anyway, after the assessment my whole world turned around and I began to read and write in ways that worked for me. I wasn't stupid, I'm actually a very intelligent and highly creative young woman. Yes, I get assistance, but that's primarily because I'm in the minority and just like Olivia, until I was assessed, I had noone to talk to about my situation because I actually believed there was something wrong with me and was too afraid to raise it with anyone for fear of being punished. My parents needing me to be perfect, even at that young age, was too much for me to handle.

In Olivia's outpouring at the Double G night, she stated that her confusion started at a young age when she was around the age of seven. Her friends started to tell her that the man she called 'Dad' wasn't because he was a different race to her and that it was not possible that he could be her dad. Olivia defended her relationship identity with her Dad because at that age she didn't know that her own father had died and that the man who'd raised her wasn't her biological parent. But the more she defended the relationship, the more her friends laughed at her. Olivia's Mum hadn't told her the truth about her paternal heritage, but the laws of nature had already been explained to some degree to her by her friends who were a little older and whose parents were discussing the matter privately in the home.

Finding out in this way devastated Olivia. She said she felt that she'd been living a lie. She felt betrayed because she was left to find out about her heritage rather than have it explained to her by the people who claimed to love her. She hadn't understood what colour was at that young age, she was blind to the differences because of the broad contrast of light brown and to dark brown skinned relatives in her own family. She wasn't the darkest in her family but neither was she the lightest. Her ability to distinguish that a dark-skinned man, who she thought was her biological father, could not in her young naive eyes be considered anything other than her Dad because she didn't at that age have a concept of step-dad or racial identity.

Joe was the only Dad she ever knew. He'd always been there but now knowing he wasn't her biological father began to make certain other things make sense. All of a sudden a colour-box of browns had become a box of suspicion.

Olivia said she responded to her friends' taunting by eventually asking her mum about the facts of life and it was as a result of Olivia asking that question that the truth behind her heritage came out. This brought about a massive crisis in identity for Olivia as well as trust issues.

Olivia went on to talk about other chapters in her life and she recalled when she turned thirteen, she was asked challenging questions about whether she preferred white boys to black boys. She being cheeky replied that she's got a thing for men with fit behinds and calls it the Path of RightAssNess! Either that or the Path of RightNastyNess. Totally crazy chic but I love me some of her humour ☺. But humour was a deflecting tactic that Olivia used under pressure.

In her reflection, Olivia stated that these were difficult and distressing questions for her to have to answer when all you want to be certain of is that you're liked by other girls and that people think you're pretty. I mean how many girls have any kind of serious relationships at this stage and age anyway? Most are more into their T.V. BoxSet Boyfriends, guys playing guys on TV dramas and getting a big-time crush on them. They talk about these people like they're real…not even the actor but the character that they play. Yep, BoxSet Boyfriends hahahahaha! Now you got to be picking a guy based on race? Allow that! At that age we weren't allowed a boyfriend let alone be thinking about what his race, class and CreedEntials are, but things are changing and the youngers are thinking about these things.

Olivia went on to share that prior to being asked

these types of questions, she was oblivious to racism but upon reflection the worst kind of racist harassment she faced so far in her life had already occurred. She went on to explain that a young person shouldn't have to think about let alone have to have an answer for dilemmas such as picking sides in a war against two racial groups. For her it was a nonsense anyway because her racial heritage stretched beyond more than two racial groups but ignorance doesn't make allowances for misfits any more than the education system makes allowances for spotting and supporting dyslexia often before it's too late.

Olivia described how the need to belong for any young person is so important at each school year age, but that for each change of school or classmates, this form of racial harassment would continue and with noone to talk to about it, that tonight at Double G was the first chance she had to share her feelings in a safe place. I had suggested to Olivia that she come along to Double G because Eva ran several sessions on the subject of identity that would help her to unravel who she is for herself, build her confidence in who she says she is rather than how other people described her.

Olivia has a very interesting family history that spans four continents. She says that the torment that she goes through, especially from us girls, usually boils down to a matter of trust. The matter of trusting an 'Other', a non-boxable other. But when she remembers her family heritage she says it helps her to remain rooted because knowledge about who she is and where she comes from is more important to her now than the desire to belong to a single group of mates. She said that it'd be simpler to tick one box that describes her but she has moved toward a higher level of understanding that has replaced her sense of confusion and embarrassment with a sense of pride and the fun side of being 'different'. She said that people still view her with suspicion or worse still as 'exotic'. She says that there are shallow people all around and if they weren't hating on her for being mixed it'd probably be for something else, for that she was sure. Her main concern that I thought was crucial, is that more and more people are having mixed heritage children but that they don't necessarily have the skills or experience to raise a child who'll face challenges that only mixed heritage children face. She celebrates different people of mixed races and some of her heroes include Alicia Keys, Bob Marley, Sophie Okonedo and Barack Obama. She feels that the more she reads of other people's lives and experiences the more she feels that she'd like to set up a support group with Eva's help.

Some of her biggest gripes have been having to explain why her hair is the way it is, her skin colour that changes many shades between the spring to summer months, the music she likes or the way that she speaks. She says how fed up she is of having to justify it, when it's ALL part of her heritage. Being enriched should never result in downplaying your blessings (a quote from Eva when Olivia started to play down her multifaceted background). It's almost like trying to define your talents and gifts down to just one. Olivia says that people picking away at her cultural heritage is like identity theft, tearing it down bit by bit, tearing down your identity until nothing of it is left, people telling you

'you're not' when you know that you ARE! People trying to describe you neatly in one tick box, when not even three could describe you. And then when she tries to insist on who she is, she's hated for it, persecuted for it, despised for it, abused and treated less than a human being with feelings. Boys that only want to treat you like a trophy on their arm, like something to boast about, seen as a thing, an object of desire, somebody's curiosity, an exotic fruit, anything but a person.

Being wanted for everything else but being a person has resulted in her being in abusive relationships. Entrapped by possessive boyfriends who treat her as their possession then beat her when they believe they're losing 'the object of their desire'. I mean I don't claim to try to get into the mindset of an insecure man, that's a diary entry for another time. But for now, all I know is that men who believe the world revolves around the value they place on material possession above human kindness, love and authenticity, are people to study much deeper before jumping straight into bed, as it were, with them. But then, here lays one of the issues that

Olivia has with her father and explains how the distance between them as father-daughter, was offset by virtue of the fact that he wasn't her biological father and there was a disconnect, not because he didn't love her but because her mother was overly protective of her having lost one father already. Olivia's mother was insecure about her relationships after losing Olivia's father to the Iraq War. Right or wrong, she kept Joe at a distance in matters to do with Olivia because in her view, she needed to be at the forefront of Olivia's life to ensure a constant security for her. Right or wrong it affected the father-daughter relationship with Olivia and Joe and as such Olivia fell in love with guys who were distant, hard to reach and often controlling like Olivia's mother.

When it comes to relationships Olivia's view is that she can't be safe with anyone because they're unable to genuinely like her for who she is on the inside. And one of the reasons why she wants to do the identity course is because she wants to stop defining herself by the way she looks and more by who she is inside. Olivia said she wants to have a deeper understanding of why people treat her in what she feels is a negative way and wants to learn to feel less defensive about herself. I cannot wait to see how Olivia is affected by Eva's Identity and Diversity sessions.

October

Oct 1   Torrie poured her heart out to us last night. I felt so emotional (pregnancy does this, it's the hormones). I really wanted to hug her. I found myself imitating Aunt Eva when she first met me at that bus-stop. I remembered how just listening was so important to me. I found my pack of Aloe Vera Handy Pack Tissues and took one for myself and gave Torrie the pack. I just had a strong urge to give. Torrie looked at my hand and I gave her my best, 'I know how you feel' look. E.M.P.A.T.H.Y. is growing in me and creating a new and beautiful relationship with others.

Oct 2   Had a one-to-one session with Eva. Talked to her about my abuse. She made an appointment for me to see a specialist counsellor. She described what I had been through as early childhood trauma. I've got three back-to-back sessions. I've already had to get an extended registration date for school. Am I even going to get to start? It's making my head hurt, it's too much to think about right now.

Oct 5   Saw the specialist for the third time. Her name is Gaia and is pronounced guy-ya. I like her and I hate her. I get angry every time we meet. But the more I get my stuff up to the surface, the more I can feel myself healing. Eva says that healing enables us to flourish into our full potential and helps us to be the best that we can be.

Oct 9   Had a miscarriage.

So how did I get to this place? I wasn't thinking was I? Breaking up with Luke devastated me. Eva called what I did with Louis the 'rebound' thing but I was just only feeling 'cyber-pretty' at the time. He looked good in his photo too and like most social media pics, the reality can be different but we both liked the real look of each other and I had no real need to fake what I looked like but I did send that soft hazy selfie pic so I guess I was trying it with the 'cyber-pretty-fake-ass-ness'.

Eva explained that feelings of rejection and abandonment can make you do that rebound thing. She explained that those feelings reminded me of when I was younger, my experiences I had as a child. I can't write about the miscarriage. It's stuck in my heart; my heart is broken once more. It's beneath the hurt of my Luke, MY LUKE! And beneath the hurt of my broken heart is my abuse which's stuck beneath my Luke and my miscarriage and all of my other crazy decisions that have got me to where I am today. I feel more than choked up inside because no matter what I really wanted, nothing comes close to the physical and emotional pain of losing a part of what was growing inside of you.

Oct 13   Eva says that even though you grow up, the child you were remains inside of you. So all of my feelings and memories stay within mini me, the child in me, the inner child. She says that if we don't realise it, that inner child when angry can drive our behaviour, our thoughts, the words we speak and cause us to do all kinds of mad, inappropriate and out of our right-mind things. She says it's not the only cause but being aware of the idea of the existence of the inner child is a smart kind of awareness. An awareness of our own immaturity for example. I'll testify to that; I've seen the adults in my life behaving like kids in adult bodies. Aren't they embarrassed by it, acting like they do in front of their children and each other? Do adults really believe that it's ok to project their unresolved, unhealed issues onto their own babies? To be neglectful as they lay wasted owing to alcoholic or some other form of substance abuse? Is that neglect ok? So it happened to them so it's ok to dole that behaviour out onto the next generation? Isn't there some notion that the next generation may well object to that abuse? That they may have the gumption, the guts, the nerve, the audacity, to take a stand and break the cycle of irresponsible, often abusive, always unacceptable behaviours of the prior generation? That they may decide to 'defend' themselves against forms of attack from their parents or people in custodial roles, including teachers? Does the title of 'parent' mean that somehow you're not accountable to your children for your behaviour? Would you rather complete strangers or the 'system' have to point that out to you before you make a change? How many adults in roles in society actually have graduated sufficiently in their own healing and well-being and can hand on heart say they don't off-load their stuff onto the young people they are supposed to be assisting?

I'm done.

Oct 14   Had a talk therapy session today to discuss the miscarriage with Aunt Eva. We talked more about how I got myself into this situation. Eva said that because my Mum and biological father had a volatile relationship that ended in violence, this had an influence in making it really hard for me to feel secure and safe. She said that one of the many things I had felt was insecurity, and that I know I was feeling this because it was usually at this point that I expressed anger and sometimes violence and a deep seated sense of impending abandonment. Feel drained, will write some more tomorrow.

Oct 15   Talk therapy sessions can leave me feeling a bit deflated sometimes. When I begin to make sense of why I do or did what I've done, it can make me both very sad and liberated at the same time. Why couldn't I have known then what I know now, can you tell me that? I push on, keep on keeping on.

Oct 19   What did I do to change the feelings of insecurity when Luke dumped me? I ain't gonna lie, social media was an outlet. Cyber fakeness allowed me to pass as something I needed to be and allowed me to get the attention I needed. I dumped those insecurities onto Louis by sleeping with him, with the aim of making me feel 'complete'. I didn't intend to sleep with him, he just wouldn't take no for an answer and one thing led to another because I was emotionally and mentally weak. I guess it's like when I met him at that rave during the summer, he was all over me like a rash and I was in need of some affection. The attention was sweet, an antidote for the hurt I felt when Luke and I ended. I dealt with my pain by generating a whole heap more.

Oct 21   The opportunity to talk to others about my various issues has taught me how to give a damn because in the past I didn't. Too many of us haven't had people in our lives who've really cared for and loved us. Some things about love can and have to be taught and thinking about others while taking care of ourselves first is an art that few people have attained. I noticed that we seem to be at extreme opposite ends of the giving spectrum, either over giving to people who don't even consider you as a choice or fuckin anything; or not giving a damn about anybody but ourselves. There must be a balance in that. Eva says we must strive to achieve the balance in all things. Achieve Maat. Scales of Justice.

Oct 25   I want to talk about the miscarriage.
The drama of it was unbelievable. Talk about pain!

And you know I don't like pain. I was at a Double G meeting and Torries was sharing her story in quite some detail. It was heart wrenching and had most of us spilling buckets of tears. I think we could all say we had to some extent or another a cathartic release listening to her plight. All of a sudden I yelled out in pain. Torrie was shocked out of her tears and the rest of the group just stared at me in shock. The pain seared through me, piercing my lower abdomen like the worse period pain ever. I noticed some dampness between my legs and stood up and the cramp caught me again. It was at this point Eva ran over to me. She immediately understood what was happening and led me into a separate room while requesting the group meeting end early that evening. The girls bid their farewells, some with tears welling in their eyes and trying through their hazy glare to show me their love and concern. Eva took me into the first aid room and led me over to the couch. I laid down but just couldn't get comfortable. I twisted and turned with the cramp tearing away at my insides with each move. I had noticed someone hovering outside after Eva said she'd go to her office to call an ambulance. It was Torrie. She looked at me seeking permission to come in. I gave her a pleading nod and she didn't hesitate to come to my aid, offering a hand to caress my tensed shoulders. She asked if I was pregnant and I nodded. She said she'd had a miscarriage and knew the signs. She held my hand and stroked my hair and this act of kindness calmed me down because unbeknownst to her it was one of those things my Mum used to do to make me sleepy and to express her love for me. When the ambulance arrived, I was wheeled out. I don't want to go into the rest of the details but all I can say is that I felt overwhelming sadness at the loss of my baby. I couldn't stop crying.

Oct 26 More to say, but I can't write it down right now. Too much emotional overload. Can't find the words. Told Louis about the miscarriage. He's relieved. He still wants us to be together but I need time for me and to give myself a chance to get to know who I am, why I'm here on this planet and what I really want. I'm learning that self-determination is not an act of selfishness. Self-determination helps us to define who we are and enables us to practice being who we are in ways that complement us. For example, I've always loved art. I'm learning to use art to draw pictures that help to describe where I want to be in the future. Aunt Eva calls this visioning. I've my own vision board on my bedroom wall and I glance at it daily and once or twice a week I tweak it by adding or replacing what's on it. I find it hard to vision sometimes because I just don't know where to start. How can I know what's possible for me in the future when I don't know what's possible? It's hard to know what's possible when I don't know what I don't know! So with the aid of discussion around economic power and money, leadership and education, I began to get a clearer picture tonight at Eva's Double G session. Eva says that it's not enough to evolve emotionally, spiritually and physically. She says that part of life on this planet requires us to be economically savvy and so she has built in a module into our sessions that enable us to consider economics at the nano and micro economy levels. This is primarily because she believes that young people are highly entrepreneurial due to their tendency to be undiluted creatives and that it should be harnessed in preparation for generating future income. She believes in the economic empowerment of young people and teaches us a variety of skills and techniques to strengthen what she calls our economic muscle. I've to say, the games we play to learn these skills are extremely good at raising our awareness around the subject matter to the point that some of the girls have started to work with organisations that assist young people in setting up their nano businesses. Part of the skill base is to be able to vision, which for me is not only about material gains like the house, car and environment that I want to live in. It's also about the kind of vibe I want my home to have, such as music, harmony, peace, happy and what I now express as spirit-filled.

Through our visioning conversations, Eva helps us to define what we want our future to look like using positive images and positive language through cutting out words from newspapers and magazines.

Words such as 'I can', 'I will', rather than 'I don't' or 'I might', or 'maybe'. She explained that talking positive has the ability to help attract positive outcomes and talking negatively can have our attention focused upon negative outcomes. What we call ourselves and others is important too. For example: 'I'm a procrastinator'. We did *a 'Who do you say you are'* session on this and we all raised our hands admitting that we procrastinate but Eva suggested we can change our behaviour by visioning different behaviour so instead of me seeing myself as a procrastinator I now see myself as a doer, a completer. Today I completed my positive affirmation. It's only short but I believe it to be powerful. Here it is:

The Sun Rises on my Sunset

Therefore

Light

Is always

On my

Horizon

Eva explained to us that positive affirmations are a way of reminding us of the positive good ideas that we have about ourselves, our present and our future. We can read them daily or listen to them if we record them (which I did) to programme positive thoughts and associated visions into our minds. This, for someone like me who couldn't even vision past today, is a big achievement. It gives me hope. I've begun to write my positive affirmation for the future and what I believe for myself starting today.

I am Candika

I am smart

I am 21 years of age and have just finished my degree in Psychology

I am good in spirit

I am in a relationship and I have no children

I am loving

I am planning a long-awaited holiday to Egypt.

Egypt is a place that feels like my spiritual home

I live in a rented apartment in south-west London

I have a miniature black Dashund that my boyfriend bought me for my 25th birthday

His name is Sherlock

I just passed my driving test and passed first time

I have an environmentally friendly economic car

I also have an electronic motor bike
I have a full-time job working for a small company
I am the company director and pay my own salary
I provide mediation services for young people
This is as far as I've got. It's a lot for me to try to imagine at the age of almost 17 and with all the chaos going on in my life. I struggle with identifying what's possible for me in the future but Eva helped me out by saying that I'm only limited by my own imagination. So the deal here is to use my imagination!

Oct 28　The cat's out of the bag and I haven't told you. Because of my age, my Mum had to be involved and she needed to be informed of my miscarriage. When Mum arrived at the hospital Eva had a long chat with her out in the corridor. Mum and I had a long overdue talk today and now I know what they talked about! My Mum had shared with Eva her own limited ability to do what she wanted in life because of having children so young and without any financial support after the death of my father. Mum's decision to keep us gave her, in her opinion, the right to deal with us in any way she wanted, which generally speaking was the way in which she was treated by her own guardians. More to come on that but I now need to shut down early tonight. I'm tired, period is due and I need my beauty sleep!

Oct 30 Mum explained to me that she'd been made promises by men who broke them. They turned out to be the wrong choices. Me, my sister and brother all have different dads, but that's another story. Mum described to me what her dreams had been and that she could never see any way forward in ever achieving the ambitions she once had. I didn't even know that my Mum had dreams and ambitions for herself and her life. She just never ever discussed that with me, not until today! ☺

Wendy McPherson

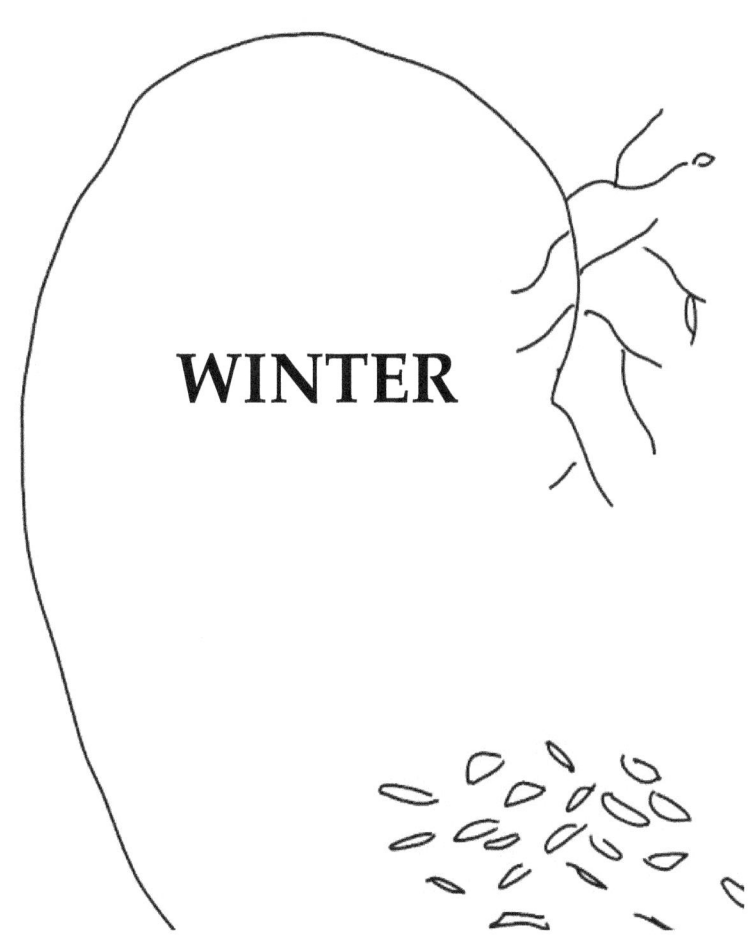

WINTER

Extracts from a Diary: Candika's Journal

November

Nov 1 Mum has just joined Eva's group for women. Very similar to Double G meetings but for adults over 35 only! Mum said that she began to notice the difference that Double G had made in me. My change in behaviour etc. Wow! That's like the child leading the adult here! Eva says that we children play a role in teaching our parents and that parent-child relationships aren't just a one-way lesson in life. That thought to me is just mind blowing! The thought that we can teach our parents a thing or two had never crossed my mind outside of discussing the latest academic lessons at school. The way the 'adult', the 'grown' people in my life behave, they spent so much time trashing me, my ideas, my dreams, my present accomplishments, that they never got to thinking that just maybe I might be doing something worthwhile. Sometimes it's not the motivation of our parents that encourage us to make a change, sometimes it can actually come through from within our own young minds. ☺

Nov 4	Mother is changing. Since joining her group she's gradually shifting in her outlook, her thoughts and her language. The most dramatic shift is the way she now communicates with me. To say that our exchanges are more respectful is an understatement and this is benefitting the whole family. But it's also causing tension between my Mum and my Stepdad Kane. This is because Mum has found her 'voice' and some of that lost ambition, and she's spending less time slouching on the sofa and finding herself more and more involved in her growing hobby – the amateur arts. Yep, she's taking up her love of acting, something she says she hasn't done since leaving school.

Nov 7	Mum lashed out at me today. Yep, the old ways are still there. Some of that poison coming out, like a mental detox. She apologised after flushing out her verbal diarrhoea, almost as soon as she had finished. Not nice feeling like the punch bag once again, but the apology? Now that is new! She's talking more softly now whenever she wants to express herself or correct me on something instead of all the shouting, screaming, raging, digging up the past, comparing me to my other siblings and all of that dysfunctional stuff.

Nov 8 Overall I'm noticing that Mum and Kane are arguing less often. She just seems to be so much more relaxed, less wound up all of the time. Most of all, she's able to talk about how she feels and what she does and doesn't want in such a way that leaves me feeling like she may actually love me. Ok that's pushing it, she may just like me. Before her sessions I had been blamed, criticised and she'd try to destroy my character – she's really into character assassination. I used to think she hated me. But now, I can listen to her more easily and because of the hard work I've done on myself through Double G and the counselling sessions, I understand myself more and how we all affect each other. I take my time to be still before I act irrationally like I did before I knew better. Yes I may still have crazy thoughts but I am getting much better at not needing to verbalise them until I've calmed down. This often changes my narrative and getting what I want to get across comes through in a much more considered way. End result? I feel like I am being listened to.

Nov 9   It's been a month since the miscarriage. Eva and I have talked about the need to properly heal. She explained to me that healing isn't just physical, it is also a mental and spiritual thing. I feel I've just begun the grieving process. With Christmas, mock exams, new years and everything all coming at the same time, I had suppressed the grieving process. Eva recommended organic Camomile Tea at bedtimes and peppermint tea for breakfast.

I'm giving more thought to nutrition and eating properly.

Joined my local fitness centre. It's free in my area to encourage young people to take up regular exercise. Obesity is such an issue and if it isn't then you've got these size zero's walking around. Since losing the baby I felt self-conscious about my body. In fact, being pregnant made me tune in to aspects of my female side I never knew about up until then. It's noticeable that my breasts have reduced back down in size. I am feeling more confident about my body image because Eva taught me the value of self-worth and that part of the poor body image is the low self-esteem that I've felt due to feeling constantly criticized by my Mum as well as other family members. Either I'm too skinny or too fat depending on who's speaking to me. Usually it's the other girls focusing on how fat I am, so fuckin what? I'm still growing and as Mum says there's still the adolescent fats to burn off. All that energy is needed for the amount of change our adolescent bodies are going through.

Nov 12   Eva brought a really good book to Double G tonight. It teaches us about making nutritional and healthy meals. I had asked Eva if she could find something for me because my parents don't do healthy eating according to my current observations and experience.

Tonight it was Harper's turn to take the Truth chair. She has been put into Local Authority care. She has finally got what she wanted, which was to get out of the mad-house. Her only regret is that it had ended up with her in foster care but according to what she shared, it looks like she has got placed with a caring couple, both of them doing the fostering rather than just the woman. Harper has been sexually molested by her uncle and her mother's ex-boyfriend. Her mum's got a new man and basically they don't have a relationship because Harper's Mum's shit scared of anything happening between them so this current boyfriend is under strict instructions to not hug her, kiss her, touch her - JUST IN CASE. As a result, they don't really have what Harper wants, which is something like a healthy father-daughter relationship, whatever that is! He's just there for her mother but not there for her. My question is, if Harper's mother is that concerned, why does she allow her boyfriend to live with her? Why doesn't she wait until Harper is an adult or leaves home? I don't get that arrangement at all and it just seems like she wants to have her cake and eat it with no real consideration for Harper's needs. She's setting the relationship between her boyfriend and her daughter to be one based upon suspicion and rivalry rather than love and trust.

Anyhoo…Harper's Mum has three children from another relationship and Harper's Dad disappeared when he found out Harper's Mum was pregnant for him (he was a married man, according to what Harper's Mum has told her). Harper is the youngest in her family, she is just 15. It's not the first time she has been in care. She went in before when she was little on account of the fact that her mother just couldn't cope with that many children all under the age of 7.

Harper's Mum had been a drug addict at the time and the substance misuse has resulted in her Mum experiencing mental health issues as well. She suffers from mood swings and one day beat the shit out of Harper's brother. It was so bad that the whole lot of them were temporarily placed in foster care until her Mum could be assessed. So now her Mum takes tablets to cope with her mood swings but her Mum's boyfriend doesn't help because he still supplies the drugs to her Mum.

Eventually Harper got back in touch with her biological father and he was awarded custody because Harper's Mum slipped back into drug use, so she has been spending time at her paternal grandmother's house. Her Dad's younger brother Connor lives at home and Harper said that one thing led to another but not full blown sex. He's just under five years older than Harper (grandmother's love child) and she said they get on really well. But Harper's aunt caught them one day and on account of the fact that she's a social worker had to report the matter to the social services.

So what exactly were they up to? Playing doctors and nurses. The thing about that game is that we all know that there's an element of curiosity that gets unveiled in that role play. Eva has spoken to us before about the sexualisation of women and women in the workplace. Nevertheless, the pair of them played out their fantasy and as Harper had got to the point of nearly stripping down to her bare essentials, her aunt walked in on them both seeing Connor bumping and grinding on top of Harper on the bed. So now the whole thing has turned into another family drama and this relative isn't speaking to the next and accusations of poor parenting flying everywhere and up and down the intergenerational ladder!

So the poor girl is back in care again but says she welcomes it because all that she wants is stability and right now, she doesn't care that it doesn't come from her own parents, she's had enough of bouncing around. Harper is a trier. She has tried so hard to keep up with her education but if I thought my life was bad, she lives a roller coaster of living in temporary accommodation with other people's family or no family at all. It makes me think seriously about what family life is really all about.

For each move she had to change schools and she never knows which social services department is responsible for her because it takes a while for each service to pass over her records to the current service provider. She's forever in transition! Can this be right in this day and age of computers, cloud services and 21st century technology? Is there a single adult in that girl's life who cares enough to assure some consistency regardless of geographical location?

Nov 15   I've been giving more thought to the idea of self-determination. I'm realising that in order to be self-determining it requires me to take ownership, responsibility, for my every action, word and decision.

Nov 16   Double G has taught me a number of skills:
Visioning
Planning
Goals setting
Identity
Values and beliefs
Positive language
Perceptions
Self-determination
Integrity
Empathy
I could go on; the growth is REAL!
Visioning techniques have allowed me to see life differently. Being able to see life differently means that I can spend less time thinking about the past, and more time devoted to planning for the future.
I've decided that personal development is an essential ingredient missing from my educational

curriculum. If Double G was a lesson taught at school, it would be WICKED!!! Every, and I mean EVERY girl and boy should be able to have access to learning these life changing skills.

We shouldn't have to wait until we get into extreme trouble before we're offered something like this. What if I hadn't seen Eva at the bus stop? I may have never heard of 'personal development' or 'process' or been 'empowered' with the techniques I've been taught. Using creativity to transfer learning is so much easier than sitting in front of a teacher who's just plain lecturing! Sitting in a circle or even a horse shoe shape would be a much more positive layout in the classroom than rows of seats. We can see each other, motivate each other and as Eva says, positively reinforce each other rather than seeing the backs of each other's heads!!! How outdated our seating preferences are for some lessons, surely there can be flexibility built into the layout of teaching spaces?

Nov 18   Low self-esteem (LoSE).

LoSE has been a major barrier in my life so far. I

lost out when LoSE is on the rampage!! It came up in my counselling session today.

I've learnt that I had very low self-esteem because I have parents who needed me to be perfect in order to make up for their own imperfections, flaws, failures and fuckedupnesses. This has worn my self-esteem down and out to a thin membrane.

Perfection, along with neglect and abuse, had turned me into a hypersensitive person with low self-confidence. This hypersensitivity made me sensitive to criticism of any kind, even if it was constructive. Taking up the arts, singing and acting especially, helped me to express myself in ways that I couldn't do before I learnt about what Eva calls 'the foundations to exceptional communication'.

Being a creative person and being able to express myself in that form, is helping me to build up my confidence and more recently I've found ways of turning my poems into songs. I've heard that song writers can earn good money through their royalties. I must look more into that and update my vision board.

Nov 22   Using my creative and artistic skills really helps me to manage my emotions when I feel myself getting hyper. I'm also tuning into music that I find very calming like Buddhist monk meditation music. I'm not a Buddhist but I do like to meditate and that kind of music is very calming and relaxing for me. I find being creative so rewarding, it's a gift to myself and I try to give in that way whenever I get the time. I'm making more time to put myself first and in being creative I get to express some love for me in this way. It's an activity that I love to do and when you do what you love to do it costs nothing and it doesn't drain my energy. In fact, quite the reverse, it energises me.

I shared this with Double G tonight and realised that I wasn't the only one with these skills, these gifts are widespread. So, with Eva's help, some of the girls and I have come together to create a social enterprise organisation where we can sell our art and craft and run classes for younger girls based on the Double G programme.

Nov 26   Eva and her colleagues have been working collaboratively with us to help develop the personal development programmes for young girls, which we are calling 'Rising Women'! Must share this with the wider group attendees to get their views. We're also developing a book based on my journal.

Nov 28   Rising Women has been born!!! Yay!!!

December

Dec 1   One of Eva's colleagues is quite influential in the education department and has a major interest in the 'Wellbeing' health agenda. We're planning a school visit roadshow to talk to schools in the borough about Rising Women. Our aim is to complete the roadshow before the Christmas break. No pressure.

Dec 3   Did our first presentation at one of the schools in the borough today. I was so nervous. I could feel it building up, the nerves beginning to immobilise me. I put my positive visioning skills into full effect in order to change the way I was feeling on the inside. I was feeling hot and clammy and my mouth was so dry I could hardly feel my tongue and I didn't want to get tongue twisted when I started to speak. I imagined that I was on stage singing one of my songs, confidently, with my head held up and seeing the audience enjoying my performance. When I went onto the stage at the school, I took that same positive image with me and it WORKED! I delivered with such confidence and got so much positive feedback, I was positively beaming like a Sunflower! It's the first time that I've spoken in public before and who would have thought that I, Candika Aasiya Lazuli Knight could do something like that. I felt so proud and most of all felt so humbled by the amount of young girls who signed up to attend our launch of the Rising Women event.

Dec 10 I've had an operation. Lost one of my fallopian tubes on account of a cyst growth. I know I tested negative for chlamydia but it's a silent disease with no presenting issues…. FFS, one down, one to go. It was blowing up like a damn air balloon. So many of our bits on the inside, so jealous of guys, they can see and feel theirs!

Dec 12   I've been reflecting. This year has been a mammoth year for turning around my outlook on life. I will turn 17 next year and I can now say that I've been given an opportunity that some may say only comes around once in a lifetime. To be honest and as traumatic as it was, falling pregnant and going through the trauma of the miscarriage provided me with an opportunity to meet an amazing woman and most of all, the chance to review my life choices and decision making. Eva is a woman who has taught me the skills and techniques for challenging and changing my mind-set and turning my life into something with purpose and into a life that I now look forward to living on a day-by-day basis. For tomorrow is not promised to us, right? It's ok to do some planning but I choose to spend each day making the most out of what's going on for me here right now. I've greatly reduced the amount of time spent drifting into thoughts about things that are and belong in the past. I can plan a little ahead and this chance I now have has me feeling grateful, not for the mistakes but for the learning opportunities that those mistakes have given me. And that has to include Janine, right? I don't like her still but she's part of the master plan and so for that reason, I give her a bly but that's all! Whether she's ever going to learn from her repeated patterns of behaviour is down to her and as for Luke, well that chapter is closed.

I feel reborn at the dawn of each new day. Thank you for you Eva.

Dec 15   Losing my fallopian tube is totally distressing me. I've been trying to deal with the whole self-hate and guilt. Self-blame and self-harming thing. I call this GBHS – Grievous Bodily Harm of the Self. And yes, it's grievous bodily harm of the mental kind, too.

Dec 17   I vented my anger on Mum this morning and the GBHS raised up its ugly head today. To really make it a home run I went ahead and also created some drama at school. Not feeling good about this at all. I slipped back into old ways and I really don't want to be that person anymore but I couldn't stop it. It seems that time of the month leaves me feeling in an emotionally weaker state and at that point, I lapse. Something to do with Pre Menstrual Tension or PMS. I must remember that about myself and find out how I can combat that. Now that I am aware of this link, I will redouble my efforts not to put myself under unnecessary pressure to be upbeat when I don't feel like it. I remembered also what Eva said about acting in integrity and being authentic about how I am really feeling. I need to be comfortable with not having to feel or be happy-clappy when I don't and when I don't it doesn't have to mean I'm down, sometimes it's just about JUST BEING. I'm not down, I'm just trying to work with where my body's hormonal cycle is at.

I notice that I feel and let people know by acting out rather than by articulating that I need some personal alone-time to touch base with my personal emotional needs and to attend to them. Even if it means just doing a bit of song writing or something, you know, using my gifts that don't drain me, my personal pick me up. But this morning I just couldn't have that time due to needing to get ready for school and I woke up late feeling physically drained with my menstrual cycle and my brother who was in the bathroom taking all damn day to shave what little bit of hair on his face - LOL. Not funny then because at the time I felt like an internal bomb had just ticked its last second. Nada, being dysfunctional isn't for me. No to that. I must strive to be authentic in all I say and do, and if I can't, say nothing – Peace Out!

Dec 18 Had a one-to-one session with Eva tonight. I shared with her what happened yesterday. She explained that old patterns of behaviours were informed by old patterns of emotions triggered by current circumstances meeting unmet needs. She said that those feelings would often throw their heads up high begging for attention and that part of growing up was about learning to recognise and dealing with that. Welcome to adulthood where I now have to own my shit and #dealwithit.

I have to say that being part of Double G has already set me on that path. Dealing with these demons, past and present, has been a very challenging battle for me because it's so much easier to do what I've always done. But if you do what you've always done, you'll get what you've always got. If I no longer want to attract what I've always got, then I need to change what I've always done to change it. And that means responding differently when the challenge arises!

Dec 20   My unwanted behaviour in some respects has been learnt behaviour. I wasn't born this way. It has been learnt and handed down generation after generation. I've lots of role models for bad behaviours and this has been a bit of a wake-up call, a rude awakening. Eva explained this to all of us at tonight's Double G. This made me sad because I had always been proud of and very protective of my family in general and safe-guarded our secrets. But I've begun to realise that loving the person doesn't mean loving their behaviours and quite a bit of my behaviour has, and in some respects, still is unlovable – I'm a work in progress, right?

I know that the intentions of my family have been good, I have to believe that's the case. But how can I be sure about it? I mean the way they've gone about doing things aren't necessarily the best way and inherited behaviour can almost seem like the tradition often seen in religious circles! I don't question it because when I do, I get shouted down or punished in some way. I've been discouraged from questioning questionable behaviour. I've been punished for being an independent thinker and challenging the status quo and rewarded for accepting the doubtful decision making, if not outright unintelligible and that spans the spectrum of adults in my life, including school teachers.

I need to unlearn old, outmoded habits and replace them with new, positive and beneficial ways of being and thinking.

Dec 21   In my family the men and women are hard drinkers. They're violent to their partners and more often than not, to their children, and that includes me. This violence isn't just physical, it's also the way I'm looked at, spoken to and most of all the callous treatment. There's a harshness and feeling of walking on eggshells most of the time. FEAR rules the day. I hate people shouting at me because that's all the communicating my parents ever do. Relentless unnecessary unwarranted noise practically every day, loud, abusive and blaming. I mean they might be a pair of peas in the same pod but they pulled each other down rather than build each other up and we've been watching this all of our childhood lives.

I've imitated this violence, I've learnt it from the people that raised me.

Dec 22   I had an interesting discussion with Eva today about one of my beliefs. I believed that love was possible in violent relationships. That violence was actually an expression of love and that without it, love was missing. This is due to the fact that most of my physical contact with my Mum has involved hating physical violence and loving physical expressions of care. So she slapped, punched and hugged me with those same hands.

So what's happened? I called Eva on the phone because I just couldn't get last night's thoughts out of my head and I had a nightmare last night because of it. The explanation Eva gave about violence and love and the confusing messages that gives now makes sense to me. I realise more than ever why I've such a very low tolerance for pain and disrespectful behaviour, whether it's physical or mental. I guess some people will absorb it, accept it and then perpetuate it but I just don't have the DNA for that, it's just not within my human make up to accept it and perpetuate it. I avoid fighting like it's the plague and when I do go there and lose my temper, which has not been often, I literally lose all sense of physical feeling so that I can easily block out the pain. This is a coping mechanism that my body has developed to ease the pain of the regular beatings, I now can say, I used to get. I also block emotional pain in the same way so I become unfeeling. This is what

I did when I miscarried my baby but this simply delayed the natural grieving process. Eva explained that my ability to detach and emotionally disconnect is a help in certain situations but that it can also be a hindrance and arrest the development of the healing processes.

I might think I'm blocking out emotional pain but that can also act as a barrier preventing me to heal from hurtful experiences.

Dec 23　Losing my sense of feeling actually frightens me. I really go into an I DON'T GIVE A FUCK mode. This isn't good for me and I shall endeavour to not consider emotional detachment as a mental choice of action as this is a delaying tactic from the pain of healing and moving on in my life. Just like when a cut is scabbing over, it can hurt, it can itch and playing around with it can cause the scab to prematurely fall off and this delays things and can leave a nasty scar or ongoing irritation to the skin tissue, raw exposure.

I want to choose full recovery and make the scarring process as minimal as possible.

Extracts from a Diary: Candika's Journal

Eva said a scar simply means you were stronger than whatever tried to hurt you. I can respect scars, even emotional ones. They tell a story.

Dec 24 I had a really frightening experience. I smoked weed that someone gave me, someone who never shares a blunt with anyone! That should have been a red flag right there. I went blind! Actually lost my eyesight. Yes, you read right my friend, I went without sight. It lasted for about half an hour or more, I couldn't see a thing. How frightening is that? Completely fucked me up, that's how. I'll never touch that stuff again, don't want nothing to do with any substance if I can't have proof of its natural organic source.

Why do I have to go to extreme ends in order to change my ways?

Dec 28 At my one-to-one today, I flicked through my journal and raised the question about extreme ends with Aunt Eva. She explained that it was to do with past experiences. I live in, what she calls, a chaotic household where tolerance of very unacceptable behaviour, compared to less chaotic families, is very high. She said that in order for someone living my lifestyle to not have any tolerance left, I have to be tested to the nth degree, the very last nerve ends! The other reason is to do with how I experience being loved and I have, in my humble opinion, a twisted outlook on this thing.

Love and Pain go hand in hand. I need to deprogramme that and reboot.

January

Jan 3   Because of my experiences I've made some unhealthy associations. I associate love with violence, hard work with sadness and depression. I've lived with alcohol and drunks and made poor choices in guys. I've been raised by people at home and taught by people in school who have poor communication skills AND I've learnt to put up with less than what I want or deserve. These are UNHEALTHY ASSOCIATIONS and my

STANDARDS ARE LOW. So Fucked UP.

They aren't good for me because eventually it'll hurt my mental wellbeing and furthermore, the great question Eva asked yesterday was: *"Candi, how much do you want to change your ways, because if you don't the question is, how much like your Mum do you want to be with your own children?"*

Right about now, TOTALLY HEAD FUCKED!

Jan 5　I've hated the way Mum treats me and my siblings but I'm hating her less now than I did in the past, so I thought that meant change was taking place naturally. Eva explained to me that while growing up this kind of stuff is programmed into my brain like the way you download data into a computer. That often when we don't have any other examples of good behaviour or role models in our lives, we believe that what we've been told about ourselves is the truth.

This is the influence that adults, not just parents, can have in our lives. We hang onto every word seeking their approval, but when criticism is the only feedback, our need for validation becomes our neediness. That neediness can play itself out into practically any and all relationships. School, work, romantic and even friendships can see the over demanding nature of some people. Attention seeking behaviour at best and narcisstic at worse. I'm studying borderline personality types and their behaviours. To be fair, I'm no psychologist but I can really see me studying this at Uni'. I think I know why I'm on this planet! LOL

Jan 7   I've always been made to believe that what I do isn't good enough so before I met Eva I had begun not to bother. I had stopped putting effort into my work because, whether I like it or not, I believed what important people in my life have told me and in my case it hasn't been very positive, I can only take so much criticism. And I'm not just talking about Mum, not everything is always down to her. I'm talking about those teachers as well. They literally moved me out of the top classes and I never really understood why but now it's much clearer, they're worried about their overall school scoring, the overall achievements and future funding. Their own prejudices and stereotypical, discriminatory decision making placed me in these class groups for their fear of me not attaining the level of performance expected of them by the school governors and the local education authority. Yep, like I said, Eva's got connections in that system and she broke that down to me in a nutshell. Been typecast like actors for the B movies, always the bridesmaid, never the bride. Killed in the first five minutes of the movie. Always the supporting act never the star of the show. Stars of the show for people who look like me usually only get to play hookers and societal fall outs. *But why and how did people who look like me even end up in those situations?* It's rarely a lifestyle choice if other options were available.

Anyhoo, the prejudicial decision making of the educational establishment has and may continue to have an impact upon my self-concept and self-esteem. My self-identity and internal self-talk will also be influenced by those decisions. So doing the deprogramming is essential if I'm to be the person I absolutely believe that I was born to be.

I will not allow anyone to rob me of my joy. I'm good enough. I don't do perfection, right now that's a bit of a tall order, but I'll strive to be the best that I can be and if perfection is found within that, then I'll be perfection in each moment. Mwah xxxx

Jan 12   Double G blew my mind tonight. It was fantastic. Will talk more about this tomorrow. I feel like a weight that has been holding me down has been lifted. Off to the gym. Yay!

Jan 13   Home! Met this guy at the gym. Hmmm! ☺

Jan 16   I was sitting in the Truth Chair the other night. Just sharing some stuff, which will become clear to me as I write. Eva said, *"Candi, do you know whose coat you're wearing tonight?"* I was dumbstruck. I felt myself getting hot as I found myself struggling to understand the question. I was puzzled. Eva does throw out these curveball questions sometimes and it usually meant I was about to learn something profound about myself. Time's slipping and running late. More later, going back to the gym. Hope that guy is there!

Jan 18   Eva is such an interesting person. She has shared quite a bit about her life with us. She's had it rough, trust me! In many ways, she has been through what I have and am still going through. I like it when Eva talks about her adventures and how she overcame the difficulties, challenges and opportunities as she prefers to call them. She also describes these as adversities and she explains how adversity has strengthened her, how she has used it to her advantage, made it work for rather than against her. She told us that she graduated from school with very few qualifications. Her home life was complicated and so she found it hard to study. She was a carer for her disabled Mum which added to her level of responsibility placed upon her at a young age. While most children were out playing, she was cooking in place of her Mum or doing some other domestic chore.

She said she became one of those adult education learners and took up studying her degrees in her 30s. She's now exactly 40 and has just completed her master's degree. Eva has become very successful. She explained how she learnt the value of complementing what she has learnt in life with what she has learnt through further academic study. She says that it has made her more marketable. And not all of her training is academic. She also did some short courses in complementary therapies and is currently in her second year studying to become a homeopath, she's studying at a college of homeopathy somewhere in London. It sounds very interesting, must look into this!

Jan 19   Eva says she's a social entrepreneur with a passion for helping others to be the best that they can be. She aims to achieve this by giving direct support to individuals who are ready for this challenge and where possible to challenge the systems that seek to prevent people from becoming their best selves. She has her own business, which is running very successfully and she does this work with us women in her spare time. She calls this 'giving back and paying it forward'. I think she said she was going to set up Double G as a registered charity or social enterprise to make it more formal and to allow us to have an input into running the organisation if we would like to take Double G more seriously as a community based business venture. Helping other women and young people is something I'm interested in doing, but first I must get myself established in my personal development. I must write up my three-year plan and then incorporate Double G within it along with Rising Women.

My To Do List is getting long!

Jan 22   I love the fact that Eva has turned out to be such a success. She gives me the hope I need to be able to apply myself into becoming the woman that I really want to be. I've decided that Eva is going to be my mentor because I think she's a good role model. I hope she says yes to this.

Jan 28   I've been a busy rabbit over the last week. I've given some further thought and want to go back over the question Eva put to me about whose coat I'm wearing.

I asked Eva what she meant by the question and she said, "Well Candi, you know how coats have different name labels on the inside?'"

I replied, "Yes." "Well," she said. "I wondered if you'd ever thought what it meant to be wearing something that you'd made with your own name on the inside." That kinda rattled my brain. I thought about all of the things I had made in Eva's art classes and how much satisfaction I got from making them, especially the handmade accessories by upcycling some of my old clothes.

Gym time!

February

Feb 2   Getting fit is making me feel so good as well as

looking good. People are beginning to see the changes in me but I can feel the changes and I'm about that change for growth lifestyle. The guy at the gym asked me out on a date. I've made it clear that I'll go as long as he understands that I need a friendship before and above anything else. He said he just came out of a relationship and didn't want anything more right now other than some genuine companionship. This sounds good to me. He's going to call me tomorrow. His name is Daniel.

Feb 6   I've learnt that through life I've been wearing the identities of other people, and I'm not just talking about shop labels or clothing designers, street brand names and such.

They put these 'labels' on me and put no thought into what they have said to me, how they have described me and how they have informed my mindset and what I've been called by others. Being told you're this or that is like name-calling, like branding sheep or cattle. It needn't be true but you eventually begin to believe it when you're called it enough. My Mum calls me lazy, so despite my efforts not to be, I became it, but just when I'm around her. Eva explained to me that this identity has been reinforced over a period of time. That as children we aim to please our parents so we begin to perform or act out the identities that we are given, even when they're negative ones and even when they're not true and not our identities to own. Eva said that I could choose to take that coat off with someone else's name in it because it didn't belong to me. It wasn't made by me and it belonged somewhere but not on my back. Phew, how enlightening it is to know that I can unload them bags with all that stuff that doesn't belong to me. Carry the load of other people's definitions of me and people like me. Carrying on legacies of intergenerational bad mouthing, name calling and degrading, unedifying messages delivered through vexatious exchanges and snide remarks.

Pause, phone call coming through.

Daniel just called, we're going bowling tonight, need to go and get myself sorted out. Yay ☺

Feb 8 — Had a talk therapy session with Eva and I raised the Truth Chair exercise and the identity question – my coats of many colours but mine! Eva explained that we can wear ourselves down by wearing coats that don't belong to us or in other words, taking on the identities that aren't in tune with who we really are. In our session we discussed peeling back the many coat 'layers', you, know the inner linings and the labels that I carried about myself.

The session today drained me. More on that tomorrow.

Feb 9 — Me and my onion skins. Eva called it *the onion skin layers*, peeling each layer back one-by-one to begin to reveal the real me. I can't tell you how both sad and exciting the process of unravelling was. I felt sad that the identities and ideas I had about myself weren't in fact all true, especially the negative ones that I've bought into. Yes, I bought it, because an important and influential person told me these things about myself. However, I'm not at all a lazy person.

Eva explained the subtle shifts, the unconscious shifts in my behaviour that sought to align itself with what I was being told about myself. To become, hoping that it would appease or please. Imagine, at the unconscious level I was actually trying to become the negative personality that I was described to be. This is personal rebellion, personal betrayal and personal self-harm. To change my naturally beautiful me in order to become the identity of what an important person preferred me to be. This is madness!

I feel cheated somehow!

Through all the talking I'm beginning to build up a deeper understanding and sense making of what Eva calls self-esteem and self-confidence. It's increasing. I can say no and not feel afraid or guilty. My need to know the details about everything is reducing and I feel less concerned about what other people have to say about me. I'm feeling a level of self-confidence and self-assuredness that I haven't experienced before. I feel and as such am beginning to act more of what feels good and natural to me. I'm loving me more and more each day. This is self-love. This is the self-love that people often talk about. ♥☐

Feb 11   My relationship with Mum is improving to a level that we haven't had before. My need of approval from her is becoming less important and at the same time my self-esteem is increasing. I'm finding that my self-approval is good enough while Mum still struggles at times to give encouraging words of support or even a compliment. The days of finding out from her what's wrong with what I'm wearing is being replaced more with approving words. I'm taking the initiative with this since Eva explained that leadership starts with me, so sometimes I've set the example where Mum's concerned because she clearly struggles with this at times. She just doesn't know how to love me through kind words, she does harshness far easier. She can be so masculine in her energy! ☹

Feb 13   Expressing myself is so much easier compared to this time last year. My communication and writing skills, which Eva teaches us to do at Double G, coupled with my growing sense of self-awareness, has improved my ability to make friends, to listen and to understand and express how I'm feeling. The result is that I'm learning to understand and manage my emotions.

I'm not anywhere near as angry a person as I used to be. I don't feel so isolated and lonely and in fact my alone-time is precious to me as is writing this diary. I feel more secure. Feeling insecure used to get me into so much beef. I could argue till I felt I had scored enough points. I was competitive to the point that I had built up a killer line that'd crush my opponent. Arguing for me became a game of chess. That feeling of 'check-mate' when your opponent is lost for words.

I've always had a good range of words from the English language because I read and I read a lot. So I'm never short of words that people I move around with have never heard of let alone understand. But it's all been a defence mechanism. Like I said, I don't like pain so I don't like to get into physical fights if I don't have to but I could deliver words that cut like a knife, but physical knives themselves ain't for me in any way shape or form.

Knives have become the number one weapon at my school and it's not a life I want to live. Nada. I don't want no man that follows that path either. I've also developed more empathy for the things that I had no time for in others or didn't even understand, especially around my Mum and her stuff. It has helped me to cope better when I struggle with dealing with my own imperfections, I'm easing up on myself more now, not beating myself up so much. I've determined that perfection is something of a destination I visualise and own for myself. I can't be someone else's definition of perfection, that's on them to find within themselves.

I'm able to express and experience some level of compassion for myself first and foremost and now for others. My judgemental eye inherited from the adult influencers is something I now critically challenge within myself in order to identify what's actually a criticism about myself, rather than the object of my gaze.

I must first look at myself in the mirror of my own reflection before raising a forefinger at another. This, Eva says, is building strength of character. She's asked us to watch a political programme and note to what extent blame is apportioned elsewhere rather than with the elected leaders.

Feb 14   So my night out with Daniel went really well I think. He didn't try anything and I feel safe being around him because he's trying to be a friend. I don't mean 'friend-zoning', I'm talking here about really getting to know each other at the mind level. There's enough mutual physical attraction to know we aren't just trying to be buddies, but the body stuff just has to wait. It's Valentine's, but we already agreed not to bother with that but just gave each other hugs. The best things in life are free! Fun, Respectful, Enthusiasm, Ethical

If we can't be friends, I ain't desperate to be with him for anything else. Friendship has to be the foundation of any relationship. A boyfriend cannot get boyfriend benefits until he has become a friend who gives friend benefits. This is new for me and this approach to starting a relationship gets a hit on the 'LIKE' button from me. He has started to send coded messages to me on his social media page but I want to keep us private for now as I believe the early stages of a relationship are better developed off the social web radar. I'm probably going to jump out of that thing soon too unless some compelling reason to stay comes up!

Wendy McPherson

SPRING

March

Mar 1 — It's the eve of my birthday and I've been reflecting over the last year. In conclusion, my future's looking much brighter. I've had a fantastic attendance record at school and I've a five-year plan! I love Rising Women and Double G has become a good personal habit! Personal well-being and the development that has come from this process has really helped me to see things so differently and I'm grateful for the day that I met Eva and the other girls, especially Torrie. Mum joining the over 35's women's group and going through her own process has meant that our relationship is more like that of a mother and daughter and when we need to, we work more like a team together, working to our strengths. Mum's so much more supportive and tolerant and she's now addressing her addiction habits. Life with her is becoming more enjoyable.

My Birthday Wish:

I want to affirm on this Birthday Eve that this next solar year I'll build upon all that I've learnt and that I'll continue to be the best that I can be by expanding my awareness and putting into practice what I've learnt. I'm not trying to go beyond my capabilities, I've got lots to work on, so, one small step at a time, one giant leap when and only when I can.

I'm getting ready to go to Eva's, she's celebrating her 10th anniversary and has invited me over to meet her wife. ☺

Extracts from a Diary: Candika's Journal

My Self Portrait

C A N D I K A

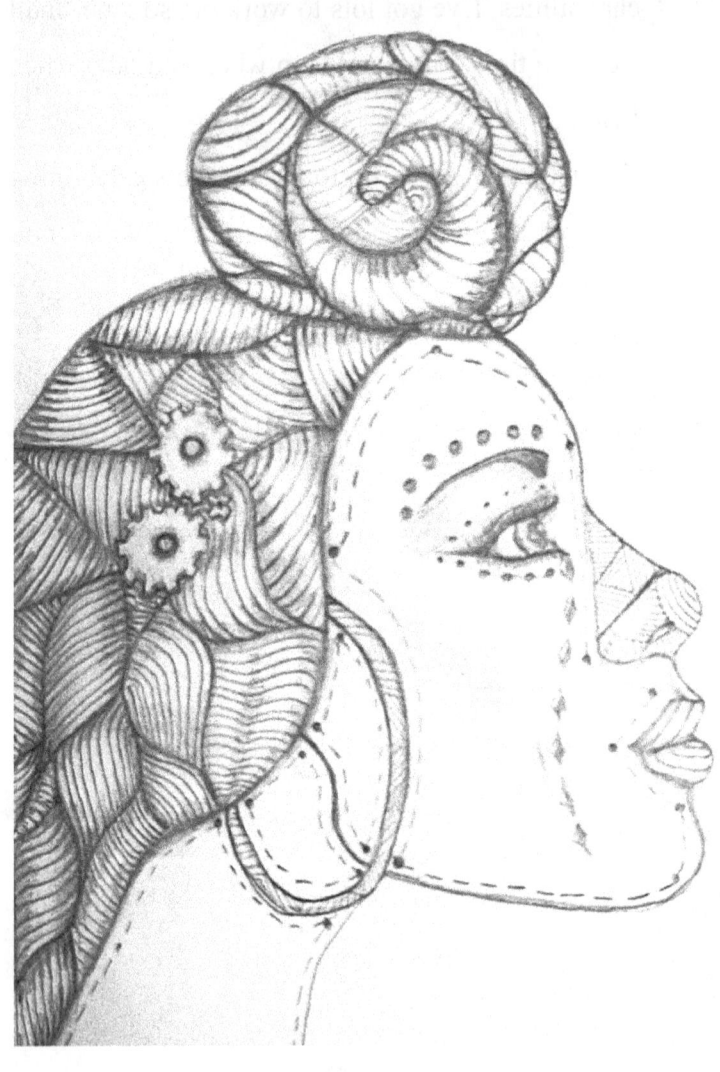

Personal Affirmation Page

_____
_____
_____
_____
_____
_____
_____
_____
_____
_____
_____
_____
_____
_____
_____
_____
_____

Signed   Dated
_____